THE
KEEP IT SHORT AND SIMPLE
COOKBOOK

Ruth H. Brent

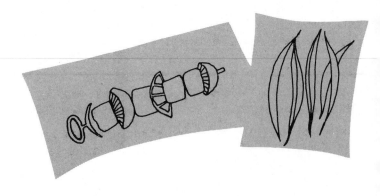

THE Keep It Short & Simple

COOKBOOK

HOLT, RINEHART AND WINSTON

New York   Chicago   San Francisco

Published simultaneously in Canada by Holt, Rinehart
and Winston of Canada, Limited.

ISBN: 0-03-086703-7
Library of Congress Catalog Card Number: 70-155506

FIRST EDITION

Designer: Margery Kronengold
Printed in the United States of America

*This book is affectionately dedicated
to my sisters, Irene and Doris,
who helped so much*

Contents

PART II.   ADDITIONAL RECIPES

Author's Note

Here is a book which every homemaker can use, whether housewife, career girl, or bachelor.

For some fifteen years I've been on a treasure hunt for a certain type of recipe. The first requirement: Each recipe must contain no more than four ingredients; the second: It must result in a delicious-tasting dish. The most important part of the search was in the preparation of each recipe in my own kitchen to make sure that it measured up to expectations. Numerous friends have helped me in my search for 3- and 4-ingredient recipes. I'd like to express my heartfelt thanks and devotion to all who helped in this way.

At one time, the more ingredients a recipe contained, the more valuable it was deemed to be. Not anymore! Few women have hours to spend in the kitchen, nor do they want to wrestle with a harrowing list of directions. There's a brand-new way of cooking. Women are taking advantage of ready-prepared and convenience foods, and are searching for new ways to use them. As an example, the average recipe for tomato aspic contains from 10 to 12 ingredients and requires the use of many kitchen utensils and the unwavering attention of the cook for a considerable period of time. The recipes in this book call for 4 or less ingredients, use few utensils, and consume little time on the part of the cook. Instead of slaving in the kitchen, she can enjoy her friends and her family and still make a tomato aspic superior in taste to that made by following most of the old recipes.

This cookbook will serve to acquaint the homemaker with the best of the convenience foods on the market. The majority of women hesitate to try new foods without the recommendation of an authority on cooking. Many women are unimaginative about food and need encouragement in incorporating time-saving devices to cut hours from meal preparations. This book will open up a new world to them.

Regarding the use of brand names: Taste and quality of various products differ a great deal. Naturally, I couldn't try all brands available, but I can guarantee the excellence of these recipes when the recommended brand is used. Another reason for mentioning certain brand names is that some products, such as Betty Crocker's packaged graham-cracker crust, are complete, whereas others call for the addition of one or two items which would push the number beyond my limit of four. No recipe in the book exceeds four main ingredients. The only ones I haven't counted are water, salt and pepper, as everyone is bound to have these items on hand.

You hold in your hands one of the best investments you'll ever make. The directions given here are short and easy to follow; the recipes are guaranteed to be delicious.

It's fun and satisfying to be a happy-go-lucky hostess in your own home. Here is the modern way of cooking for the modern woman.

Ruth H. Brent

Downey, California
June 1971

PART I Twelve Complete Menus

1

MENU

Cream-of-corn Soup

BAKED HAM SLICE

Mustard Ring Mold

Sweet-potato Fluff   Escalloped Cauliflower

Hawaiian Ambrosia

CREAM-OF-CORN SOUP

3 ingredients

SERVES 4

1 16-oz. can creamed corn
3 cups milk
4 tbsp. sour cream

Method:
1. Heat corn and milk together. Season with salt and pepper.
2. Ladle into soup bowls, then top with a dollop of sour cream.

BAKED HAM SLICE

4 ingredients

SERVES 4

2 center-cut slices ham, ¾″ thick
8 whole cloves
1 cup brown sugar
1 cup ginger ale

Method:
1. Place ham slices in 9 x 13-inch baking dish.
2. Insert cloves in fat.
3. Sprinkle brown sugar over ham.
4. Pour ginger ale around ham.
5. Bake at 350° for 40 minutes.

Note: If assembled and refrigerated ahead of time, increase baking time to 50 minutes.

MUSTARD RING MOLD

4 ingredients

SERVES 4

    1 pkg. unflavored gelatin
1½ cups cole slaw dressing (I use Kraft.)
    ½ cup dry mustard
    1 pt. heavy cream

Method:
1. Empty gelatin into top of double boiler.
2. Slowly add dressing.
3. Add mustard and stir. Cook until hot and gelatin is melted.
4. Cool.
5. Whip cream and fold in. Refrigerate until set (2–3 hours).

May be made ahead and stored in refrigerator.

Note: This is an excellent accompaniment to ham or beef entrées.

SWEET-POTATO FLUFF

4 ingredients

SERVES 4

    4 medium sweet potatoes or yams
    ½ cup brown sugar
1–1½ cups milk
10–12 pecan halves

Method:
1. Cook potatoes in boiling salted water until tender.
2. Drain, peel and mash. Add sugar and milk.
3. Beat until fluffy.

4. Pile lightly in shallow greased casserole or cake pan and arrange pecan halves over top.
5. Bake at 350° for 20 minutes.

May be made ahead and stored in refrigerator. Reheat for 20–30 minutes just before serving.

ESCALLOPED CAULIFLOWER

3 ingredients

SERVES 4

2 pkg. frozen cauliflower
2 cups milk
1 cup stuffing mix (I use Kellogg's Croutettes.)

Method:
1. Cook cauliflower in milk over medium heat until just tender.
2. Add stuffing mix to thicken and flavor.

HAWAIIAN AMBROSIA

4 ingredients

SERVES 4

1 16-oz. can tropical fruit salad, drained (I use Del Monte), or 2 cups fresh fruits may be used
1 cup shredded coconut
1 cup miniature marshmallows
1 cup sour cream

Method:
1. Toss ingredients together gently.
2. Refrigerate, covered, for several hours or overnight.

Note: This is an excellent accompaniment to open-faced sandwiches, served at a tea or reception.

2

MENU

Frosty Blender Vichyssoise

PIQUANT SWISS STEAK

Green-bean Casserole

Chocolate-wafer Mousse

FROSTY BLENDER VICHYSSOISE

4 ingredients

SERVES 4

1 10-oz. pkg. frozen creamed peas with onions
1 10½-oz. can condensed, undiluted cream-of-chicken soup
2 cups mashed potatoes (Leftovers may be used.)
2 cups milk

Method:
1. Cook creamed peas and onions according to directions.
2. Add remaining ingredients.
3. Run in blender a few moments until smooth.
4. Chill thoroughly before serving.

May be made ahead and stored in refrigerator.

PIQUANT SWISS STEAK

4 ingredients

SERVES 4

2 lbs. round or Swiss steak, cut 1½ to 2 inches thick
3 tbsp. vegetable oil or margarine
1 1⅜-oz. pkg. spaghetti sauce mix with mushrooms (I use French's.)
2 8-oz. cans tomato sauce

Method:
1. Brown meat well in hot oil or margarine.
2. Place in baking dish.
3. Combine spaghetti sauce mix and tomato sauce with pan drippings. Heat and pour over meat.
4. Bake at 350° until fork-tender (about 2 hours).

GREEN-BEAN CASSEROLE

4 ingredients

SERVES 4

1 16-oz. can French-style green beans
1 10½-oz. can condensed cream-of-mushroom soup
1 cup milk
½ 3½-oz. can French fried onions

Method:
1. Drain green beans.
2. Combine mushroom soup and milk.
3. Add soup mixture to green beans and pour into buttered baking dish.
4. Top with French fried onions.
5. Heat for 30 minutes in 350° oven until bubbly.

CHOCOLATE-WAFER MOUSSE

4 ingredients

SERVES 4

1 pt. heavy cream
1 tbsp. confectioners' sugar
½ tsp. vanilla
1 8½-oz. box chocolate wafers (I use Nabisco's "Famous Chocolate Wafers," available in cookie section of market.)

Method:
1. Whip cream.
2. Add sugar and vanilla to whipped cream.
3. Spread one side of each wafer with a thick coat of whipped cream. Stack wafers one on top of the other.
4. Lay stack in a refrigerator tray. Fill in any empty space with whipped cream.
5. Freeze several hours or overnight. (The wafers and cream blend together to make a delicious dessert.)
6. Heap in sherbet glasses to serve, or slice diagonally and serve on dessert plate.

3

ℳENU

Salade Niçoise

CHEESY CHICKEN

Oven-browned Potato Fans

Caramel-Nut Ice-cream Balls

SALADE NIÇOISE

4 ingredients

SERVES 4

1 6-oz. jar artichoke hearts
1 cup pitted ripe olives
1 3-oz. can mushrooms
1 cup bottled clear Italian dressing (I use Kraft.)

> *Optional:* Various canned vegetables—green or wax beans, small whole beets, sliced water chestnuts, etc.—may be substituted or added, as well as small chunks of tuna fish.

Method:
1. Combine first three ingredients.
2. Add dressing and marinate in refrigerator for several hours, or overnight.
3. Serve on romaine or Boston lettuce if desired.

Note: Wonderfully convenient for a party salad as it is made well in advance.

CHEESY CHICKEN

4 ingredients

SERVES 4

4 chicken breasts, split to make 8 pieces
¼ lb. margarine
1 10½-oz. can cream-of-chicken soup
2 cups grated sharp Cheddar cheese

Method:
1. Brown chicken in margarine in skillet, over medium heat. (Season to taste, if desired, but note that both soup and cheese are salty.)
2. Arrange in single layer in roasting pan.
3. Add chicken-soup mixture, diluted with 1 can water, to pan drippings and cook over low heat to make a gravy, stirring constantly.
4. Spoon gravy over chicken.
5. Sprinkle with grated cheese.
6. Bake for 1 hour at 300° until chicken is fork-tender.

May be made ahead and stored in refrigerator. Reheat for 30 minutes at 325° just before serving.

OVEN-BROWNED POTATO FANS

3 ingredients

SERVES 4

2 large boiling potatoes
½ cup melted butter
1 tsp. seasoned salt (I use Lawry's.)

Method:
1. Cut peeled potatoes in half lengthwise.
2. Place potatoes flat side down on cutting board and make cross slices about halfway through.
3. Transfer potatoes to greased baking dish.
4. Combine melted butter and seasoned salt and pour over potatoes, being sure to let the melted butter run between slices.
5. Bake until browned (about 1 hour at 300°). Spoon the melted butter over potatoes occasionally.

CARAMEL-NUT ICE CREAM BALLS

3 ingredients

SERVES 4

1 qt. vanilla ice cream
1 cup finely chopped walnuts
1 12-oz. can caramel sauce

Method:

1. Make large snowballs of ice cream with scoop or spoon and quickly roll each in chopped nuts. Place each in low dish.
2. Pour caramel sauce over ice cream and serve.

4

MENU

Spinach-Bacon Salad

CHEESE CASSEROLE

Piquant Italian Beans

Cherry Graham-cracker Pudding

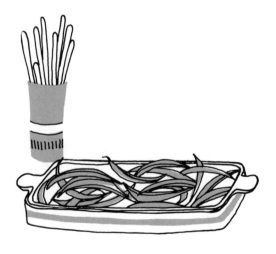

SPINACH-BACON SALAD

4 ingredients

SERVES 4

1 10-oz. pkg. fresh spinach
1 medium head fresh cauliflower
½ sweet Bermuda onion
½ cup bottled bacon dressing (I use Lawry's Canadian Bacon Flavored Dressing.)

Method:
1. Wash spinach carefully and dry on paper towels.
2. Separate cauliflower into buds.
3. Cut onion into very thin slices and separate into circles.
4. Toss lightly together spinach, cauliflower, and onion rings.
5. Heat bacon dressing at the last minute and pour over salad. Serve warm.

Note: The vegetables may be prepared ahead of time and stored in a plastic bag in refrigerator. Remove an hour before serving time.

CHEESE CASSEROLE

4 ingredients

SERVES 4

4–6 eggs (or enough to fill 1 cup)
1 10-oz. pkg. sharp Cheddar cheese (I use Kraft's Cracker Barrel, extra sharp.)
4 cups cubed bread (approx. 8 slices)
2 cups milk

Optional: 4 tbsp. bacon-onion bits (I use Lawry's Baconion.)

Method:
1. Beat eggs.
2. Grate cheese.
3. Remove crusts from bread and discard. Cut bread into ½-inch squares. An easy way is to stack the bread slices, then cut through all of them at one time.
4. Heat milk. Add eggs, bread, cheese, and Baconion, if desired.
5. Pour into greased baking dish or an 8 x 8-inch cake pan. Refrigerate several hours or overnight.
6. Bake at 325° for about 30 minutes, or until custard is set. Don't overcook.

Note: When doubling this recipe for a crowd, a 9 x 13-inch baking dish is just right. Allow 10–15 minutes extra cooking time.

PIQUANT ITALIAN GREEN BEANS

3 ingredients

SERVES 4

2 pkgs. frozen Italian green beans
4 tbsp. butter
½ tsp. Italian seasoning (I use Durkee's, available in spice and herb section of market.)

Method:
1. Cook beans according to package directions.
2. Drain. Add butter and seasoning.

CHERRY GRAHAM-CRACKER PUDDING

4 ingredients

SERVES 4

1 3⅝-oz. pkg. vanilla pudding mix
2 cups milk
1 17-oz. can dark sweet cherries, well drained and
    pitted (I use Del Monte. Other canned or fresh
    fruits may be used.)
10 graham crackers, broken into bite-sized pieces

Method:
1. Prepare pudding with milk according to directions on package.
2. Fold in gently cherries and graham-cracker pieces.
3. Chill until serving time (2 hours or more).

5

$\mathcal{M}ENU$

Waldorf Salad

ESCALLOPED HAM

AND POTATOES

Tiny Cheese Biscuits

Pecan Puffs

WALDORF SALAD

4 ingredients

SERVES 4

2 cups pared diced apples
1 cup chopped celery
½ cup chopped walnuts
½ cup bottled cole slaw dressing (I use Kraft.)

Method:
1. Combine ingredients.
2. Chill for 30 minutes before serving.

Note: Serve on lettuce leaf, if desired.

ESCALLOPED HAM AND POTATOES

4 ingredients

SERVES 4

4 medium potatoes
2 1-inch thick slices center-cut ham*
1 cup chopped onions
4 cups (approx.) milk

* These large choice center slices are usually sold separately. Slices of canned ham may be used.

Method:
1. Peel and slice potatoes.
2. Cut ham into serving pieces.
3. Place ham on bottom of greased casserole.
4. Make a layer of chopped onion, add potatoes, and cover with milk.

5. Bake, covered, in 325° oven for 1¼ hours.
6. Uncover and continue baking for 15 minutes, or until potatoes are slightly browned.

May be made ahead and stored in refrigerator. Reheat at 300° for 20–30 minutes before serving.

TINY CHEESE BISCUITS

2 ingredients

YIELD: 20 biscuit halves

1 8-oz. tube refrigerator buttermilk biscuits (I use Pillsbury.)*
2 cups grated sharp Cheddar cheese

* These biscuits come rolled in tubelike packages, 10 to a package. They must be kept refrigerated. Never freeze!

Method:
1. Cut each biscuit in half.
2. Roll in finely grated cheese. Place on cookie sheet.
3. Bake in 375° oven until biscuits are slightly brown and cheese is melted.

PECAN PUFFS

4 ingredients

YIELD : 3 dozen cookies

½ lb. butter
1½ cups confectioners' sugar
2 cups all-purpose flour
1 cup chopped pecans

Method:

1. Soften butter.
2. Beat together butter and 1 cup of sugar until light.
3. Add flour and nuts. To get this thoroughly mixed you will probably have to work it with your hands as if you were kneading dough.
4. Pinch off small pieces of dough and roll between the palms of your hands into balls the size of a walnut. Place on cookie sheet.
5. Bake at 350° for 20–30 minutes.
6. When almost cool, shake cookies in bag containing the remaining ½ cup of sugar if desired.

6

ℳENU

Guacamole Salad or Dip

SHRIMP NORFOLK

Mustard Sauce

Popovers

Upside-down Peach Cobbler

GUACAMOLE SALAD OR DIP

3 ingredients

SERVES 4

1 ripe tomato
2 ripe avocados
2 tbsp. onion-soup mix (I use Lipton.)

Method:
1. Peel tomato and avocados.
2. Mash together avocados, tomato, and soup mix, or use electric blender.
3. Chill several hours or overnight.

Note: If using as a salad, serve on lettuce.

If using as dip, add 1 or 2 tablespoons of mayonnaise for softer consistency. Very nice served with Fritos, Taco Chips, Ritz crackers, or potato chips.

SHRIMP NORFOLK

4 ingredients

SERVES 4

1½ lbs. fresh shrimp
¼ lb. butter
1 tsp. sugar
½ tsp. lemon-pepper marinade (I use Lawry's.)

Method:
1. Shell and devein shrimp. (Fresh, raw shrimp are grayish-green and soft before being cooked.)
2. Wash in cold water. Lay uncooked shrimp on several thicknesses of paper towels. Cover with additional towels to dry thoroughly.
3. Melt butter in large skillet. When sizzling, add shrimp. Sprinkle with sugar and lemon-pepper marinade.
4. Cook for 3 or 4 minutes, turning all the while, until shrimp turn pink, are firm to the touch, and are slightly browned. Serve piping hot with mustard sauce (see following recipe).

MUSTARD SAUCE

4 ingredients

YIELD: ¾ cup

½ cup sugar
½ cup dry mustard (or less if you prefer a milder sauce)
2–3 eggs (or ¾ cup)
½ cup vinegar

Method:
1. Mix together sugar and mustard.
2. Beat eggs, add to above mixture, and stir until smooth.
3. Dilute vinegar with ½ cup of water, combine with other ingredients, and mix well.
4. Cook on medium-high burner, stirring constantly, until thick.
5. Store in refrigerator.

Note: A very appetizing sauce, excellent with ham, cold cuts, or cold roast beef. As a fish sauce, I mix it half and half with ketchup (I use Heinz).

POPOVERS

4 ingredients

YIELD : 8 to 10

2 eggs
1 cup milk
1 cup flour
1 tsp. butter for each custard cup*

> * Oven-proof custard cups, so essential to this recipe, are available in most department-store household departments, or at many dime stores for a nominal sum.

Method:
1. Beat eggs lightly, then mix with milk.
2. Add flour and beat only until mixture is free from lumps.
3. Heat custard cups in oven until very hot. Remove them to counter, add butter. When melted, pour in batter until cups are almost half filled.
4. Bake for 50 minutes in a 400° oven. Remove from oven and cut slit in side of each to let steam escape. Return to oven and bake for an additional 10 minutes. Remove from cups immediately so that bottoms do not steam. Serve at once piping hot.

UPSIDE-DOWN PEACH COBBLER

3 ingredients

SERVES 4

1 9-oz. box white cake mix
1 21-oz. can peach fruit filling (I use Wilderness or Comstock.)

Optional: cream or ice cream

Method:

1. Grease 12-inch-square cake tin. Pour in peach filling.
2. Make cake batter according to directions on package.
3. Pour batter over fruit.
4. Bake until toothpick comes out clean. (This may be slightly longer than directions indicate because of the moist filling.)
5. Serve warm, either plain or topped with cream or ice cream.

7

$\mathcal{M}$ENU

GLORIFIED FRANKFURTERS

Dutch Red-Cabbage-and-Apple Casserole

Hot German Potato Salad

Pear Surprise

GLORIFIED FRANKFURTERS

4 ingredients

SERVES 4

1 10-oz. pkg. sharp Cheddar cheese
8 frankfurters
8 tsp. hamburger relish (I use Heinz.)
8 strips bacon

Method:
1. Cut cheese into strips about half the width of a frankfurter.
2. With a sharp knife, make a slit in each frank, about ¾ through.
3. Insert a strip of cheese in each slit. Spread a teaspoon of hamburger relish on cheese.
4. Wrap each frank with a piece of bacon spirally. Secure each end with a toothpick.
5. Lay frankfurters on cookie sheet, then broil about 6 inches from flame until bacon is cooked and crisp. Takes approximately 5 minutes on each side.
6. If assembled and refrigerated ahead of time, increase broiling time to 7 minutes on each side.

DUTCH RED-CABBAGE-AND-APPLE CASSEROLE

4 ingredients

SERVES 4

1 head red cabbage
6 tart apples
¼ cup sherry or wine vinegar
¼ cup maple syrup

Method:
1. Shred cabbage.
2. Cook cabbage in boiling water for 10 minutes.
3. Pare, core, and slice apples. Add to cabbage. Cook for 10 minutes more with pan covered.
4. Drain and place in buttered casserole.
5. Mix sherry (or vinegar) and syrup together and stir into cabbage mixture. Season to taste.
6. Reheat in 350° oven for about 20 minutes, or until bubbling hot.

HOT GERMAN POTATO SALAD

4 ingredients

SERVES 4

¼ lb. bacon
4 potatoes (new, boiling potatoes preferred)
1 tbsp. finely chopped onion
1 cup cole slaw dressing (I use Kraft.)

Method:
1. Fry bacon until crisp, then crumble.*
2. Boil 4 potatoes in their jackets. Peel and slice while still hot.
3. Cook onion until soft in bacon fat. Discard fat.
4. Combine potatoes, bacon, and onions.
5. Heat dressing and pour over mixture. Serve hot.

* When a recipe calls for cooked, crumbled bacon, put your kitchen shears to use. Separate the amount of bacon called for and with scissors cut crosswise into 1-inch strips. Fry, stirring all the while, until crisp. Drain on paper towels.

PEAR SURPRISE

3 ingredients

SERVES 4

4 large pear halves (canned) or 8 small ones
½ cup sour cream
4 tbsp. shaved sweet chocolate

Method:
1. Place each pear half in a sherbet glass.
2. Fill center of each with sour cream (about 1 rounded tbsp.).
3. Sprinkle shaved chocolate on top.
4. Chill in refrigerator for several hours.

8

MENU

Cranberry-mold Salad

CORNISH GAME HENS

AND RICE

Scalloped Onions with Peanut Topping

Lemon-gelatin Pound Cake

CRANBERRY-MOLD SALAD

4 ingredients

SERVES 4

½ cup canned crushed pineapple, well drained
1 3-oz. pkg. lemon gelatin
½ cup celery, cut fine
1 cup canned thick cranberry sauce, either whole-berry or jellied type

Method:
1. Drain pineapple well.
2. Dissolve gelatin in 1½ cups hot water. Set in refrigerator.
3. When slightly thickened, add celery, pineapple, and cranberry sauce.
4. Turn into mold. Chill until firm.

Note: Top with mayonnaise for salad or serve plain as relish.

CORNISH GAME HENS AND RICE

4 ingredients

SERVES 4

1 cup long-grain rice
½ pkg. Italian salad dressing mix (I use Schilling's.)
1 10½-oz. can condensed cream-of-chicken soup, undiluted
2 Cornish game hens

Method:
1. Spread rice in 9 x 13-inch baking dish and bake for 15 minutes at 375° stirring occasionally until golden brown.
2. Combine salad dressing mix with 2 cups boiling water and chicken soup, then stir into rice.

3. Cut game hens in half, lengthwise.
4. Place game hens cut side down on top of rice.
5. Bake at 350° for 1 hour. (If the hens begin to brown too quickly, cover loosely with foil.)

SCALLOPED ONIONS WITH PEANUT TOPPING

3 ingredients

SERVES 4

2 pkgs. frozen creamed onions
½ cup finely chopped peanuts
1 cup cracker crumbs (I use saltines or you may use packaged cracker meal.)

Method:
1. Cook onions according to directions on package. Turn into buttered casserole.
2. Mix peanuts with cracker crumbs, and sprinkle over top of onions.
3. Bake for 20 minutes at 350°.

LEMON-GELATIN POUND CAKE

4 ingredients

SERVES 6 to 8

1 18.5-oz. pkg. white cake mix (I use Betty Crocker.)
1 3-oz. pkg. lemon-flavored gelatin, mixed with ⅔ cup cold water
⅔ cup vegetable oil, such as Wesson or Mazola corn oil
4 eggs

Optional: 1 tsp. lemon extract or grated lemon rind

Method:
1. Mix first three ingredients together, preferably in electric mixer set at medium speed.
2. Beat in eggs, one at a time.
3. Grease and then flour large angel-food tube pan. Pour in batter and bake at 350° for 1 hour, or until toothpick comes out clean.

9

$\mathcal{M}ENU$

Tangy Grated-Cabbage-Cucumber Salad

GOLDEN FISH FRY ALMONDINE

Potato Croquettes

Raspberry Mold

TANGY GRATED-CABBAGE-CUCUMBER SALAD

4 ingredients

SERVES 4

2 cucumbers
1 small cabbage
½ 8-oz. bottle Italian dressing (I use Kraft.)
1 tsp. dried dill

Method:
1. Peel and grate cucumbers. Drain well on paper towels.
2. Grate cabbage.
3. Several hours before serving, mix all ingredients and chill in refrigerator. The flavor is improved through marinating.

Note: This is an excellent salad to serve with fish. The pungent flavor is refreshing and it's a blessing to be able to make it in advance.

GOLDEN FISH FRY ALMONDINE

4 ingredients

SERVES 4

2 16-oz. pkgs. frozen fillets such as cod, halibut, flounder, etc.
1½ cups cracker crumbs (I use saltines or packaged cracker meal. I use Nabisco.)
¼ lb. butter or margarine
¾ cup sliced, blanched almonds

Method:
1. Thaw frozen fish. Pat dry. Separate into fillets.
2. Shake fillets in bag with cracker crumbs and salt and pepper if desired.
3. Fry fillets gently in half the butter, about 3 minutes on each side until light gold in color. Remove to oven-proof serving dish. Keep hot in oven.
4. Melt remaining butter in skillet. Add almonds and brown slightly, stirring constantly. Pour sauce over fish. Run under broiler for a minute or two, or until bubbling hot. Serve at once.

POTATO CROQUETTES

3 ingredients

SERVES 4

2 cups leftover mashed potatoes, chilled (for ease of handling)
1 tsp. seasoned salt (I use Lawry's.)
1 cup cornflake crumbs

Method:
1. Add seasoned salt to mashed potatoes, and divide into 4 portions. Roll each into shape of ball. Shake in bag with cornflake crumbs until well covered.
2. Pinch top of each ball and flatten bottom so that it will be in form of croquette (cone-shaped).
3. Place on baking sheet and bake at 350° for 30 minutes until piping hot.

Note: These are great for parties as they may be made the day before, refrigerated unbaked, then baked just before serving time.

RASPBERRY MOLD

3 ingredients

SERVES 4

1 3-oz. pkg. raspberry gelatin
1 cup sweet white wine
1 cup whole raspberries

Optional: whipped cream

Method:
1. Dissolve gelatin in 1 cup hot water. Cool.
2. Add wine. Chill until syrupy.
3. Fold in raspberries. Turn into mold. Chill until firm. Unmold.
4. Serve plain or with whipped cream as topping.

10

MENU

BARBECUED SHISH KABOBS

Pilaff

Shoestring Eggplant

Persian Delight Confections

BARBECUED SHISH KABOBS

4 ingredients

SERVES 6

Bottled garlic-oil salad dressing (I use Kraft.)
Leg of lamb, cut into 1-inch squares (Your butcher
will do this.) Allow 4–6 pieces per serving.
3 green peppers
6 small, firm tomatoes

Method:

1. Pour enough tart dressing over lamb pieces to cover them.
Marinate for several hours.
2. Clean peppers and cut into bite-sized squares (each pepper
yields about 8 pieces).
3. Cut tomatoes into 4 wedges each.
4. Alternately string lamb, tomato wedges, and pepper squares
on each skewer.
5. Barbecue until meat is brown on the outside and faintly pink
inside, like a medium steak, about 5 minutes on each side. Cut
into a square of lamb to test color.

PILAFF

4 ingredients

SERVES 6

2 tbsp. instant minced onion
3 tbsp. butter
1½ cans (10½-oz.) consommé
1½ cups long-grain rice

Optional: ½ cup toasted, blanched almonds

Method:
1. Sauté onion in butter about 5 minutes, or until light brown in color.
2. Add consommé and bring to boil. Add ⅔ cup water.
3. Pour rice into greased baking dish.
4. If desired, sprinkle almonds over rice.
5. Pour consommé-onion mixture over rice.
6. Bake at 400° for 25 minutes.

SHOESTRING EGGPLANT

4 ingredients

SERVES 6

> 1 small eggplant
> 1 cup vegetable oil (I use Wesson.)
> 1 egg, mixed with 1 tbsp. water
> 1½ cups packaged cracker crumbs, sometimes referred to as cracker meal (I use Nabisco.)

Method:
1. Pare and cut eggplant into ½-inch slices, then cut slices into ½-inch strips.
2. Soak in iced, salted water for 30 minutes.
3. Drain carefully on paper towels, then pat dry.
4. In large skillet or Dutch oven heat oil to 365°, or until a bread cube will brown in 40 seconds. An electric deep fat fryer or frying pan is perfect for this job as you can maintain heat automatically.
5. Dip strips of eggplant, a few at a time, in egg mixture.
6. Place in paper bag containing cracker crumbs and shake until coated thoroughly.
7. Shallow-fry eggplant until golden brown.
8. Drain on paper towels, and sprinkle with salt if desired.

PERSIAN DELIGHT CONFECTIONS

4 ingredients

YIELD : 3 dozen

   1 cup applesauce
   1 3-oz. pkg. fruit-flavored gelatin (I use raspberry for
      both flavor and color.)
   2 cups sugar
   ⅔ cup chopped walnuts

Method:
1. Heat applesauce. Dissolve gelatin in it.
2. Add 1 cup of sugar (reserve remainder for coating). Stir over
   low heat until dissolved.
3. Add nuts, then pour into 9 x 5 x 3-inch greased loaf pan.
4. Refrigerate until firm.
5. Cut into small squares. Roll in sugar. Refrigerate. Sugar again
   after 24 hours.

11

MENU

Luncheon

BROILED BACON-WRAPPED BURGERS

Flavorful Tomato Aspic

Applesauce Quickie

BROILED BACON-WRAPPED BURGERS

3 ingredients

SERVES 4

2 tbsp. butter
1½ lbs. ground round steak*
4 slices bacon

> * Choose a piece of round steak or chuck and ask the
> butcher to grind it for you fresh. There's all the difference
> in the world between the flavor of this as opposed to buy-
> ing ready-ground meat in the market.

Method:
1. Melt butter in skillet, over medium-high heat.
2. Combine ground steak and melted butter in a bowl. Season if desired with salt and pepper.
3. Shape into patties about 1-inch thick and 3 inches in diameter.
4. Wrap a piece of bacon around the outer edge of each patty and secure ends with toothpick.
5. For medium rare, broil about 4 minutes each side.

May be made ahead of time; refrigerate until ready to broil.

FLAVORFUL TOMATO ASPIC

4 ingredients

SERVES 4

½ cup bottled low-calorie Russian dressing (I use Wishbone.)
1 cup tomato juice (I use Libby or Glorietta.)
1 pkg. unflavored gelatin (I use Knox.)
1 head Boston or romaine lettuce

Optional: Roquefort dressing or prepared onion dip

Method:
1. Heat together dressing and tomato juice.
2. Sprinkle gelatin on 2 tablespoons water to soften, then add to hot mixture and stir well.
3. Pour into 1-qt. greased mold. Chill in refrigerator for several hours until well set.
4. Serve plain on lettuce or top with Roquefort dressing or onion dip.

   Note: To add a gourmet touch, top with two or three freshly cooked shrimp.

APPLESAUCE QUICKIE

4 ingredients

SERVES 4

   2 cups sweetened, thick applesauce
   12 graham crackers
   1 cup Cool Whip (This is prepared low-calorie whipped cream found in the frozen foods department in the market.)
   ½ cup chopped walnuts

Method:
1. Put 2 or 3 tablespoons applesauce between graham crackers, allowing stack of three crackers per serving. Place on dessert plates. Top each with applesauce.
2. Place in refrigerator for several hours or overnight.
3. When ready to serve, top with whipped cream and sprinkling of nuts.

12

MENU

Sunday Breakfast

Fresh Pineapple Nibblers

E G G S   B E N E D I C T

Crisp Potato Pancake

Cinnamon Apple Rings

FRESH PINEAPPLE NIBBLERS

2 ingredients

SERVES 4

1 fresh pineapple
2 cups confectioners' sugar

Optional: 1 box strawberries

Method:
1. Lay fresh pineapple on its side. With sharp knife cut pineapple in two, lengthwise. (Be sure to leave crown attached to the pineapple. This is what makes the dish so pretty.) Cut again, making four sections.
2. With serrated knife, cut out meaty section, leaving shell intact. Remove pithy center.
3. Cut remainder into 1-inch cubes. Insert toothpick into each cube. Replace cubes in pineapple shells. Arrange sections on a plate or platter with a bowl of confectioners' sugar for dunking purposes.

May be prepared ahead of time.

Note: When strawberries are in season, they may be arranged on the same plate, leaving stems on.

EGGS BENEDICT

4 ingredients

SERVES 4

1 10½-oz. can condensed cream-of-mushroom soup
2 English muffins
8 pieces Canadian bacon
4 eggs

Method:
1. Dilute soup with ¾ cup water.
2. Split muffins, toast them, then cut each half into 8 wedges, trying to keep shape intact. Place ½ muffin in individual baking dish.
3. Cover each with 2 pieces of Canadian bacon.
4. Make a small hollow in center, then break egg into it.
5. Spoon over top ½ cup mushroom soup mixture.
6. Bake at 350° for 12–15 minutes. Eggs should be set, but not hard-cooked. They will continue cooking a little after being removed from oven.

CRISP POTATO PANCAKES

4 ingredients

SERVES 4

1 egg
2 cups leftover mashed potatoes
1 tbsp. butter or margarine
1 tbsp. seasoned salt (I use Lawry's.)

Method:
1. Beat egg slightly.
2. Stir potatoes and egg together.
3. Melt butter in heavy skillet until hot, but not smoking.
4. For each pancake, drop tablespoon of batter into hot skillet. Sprinkle with seasoning.
5. Turn when brown and firm.

FRIED APPLE RINGS

3 ingredients

SERVES 4

2 large baking apples
4 tbsp. butter
4 tbsp. cinnamon sugar (I use Schilling's.)*

> * Cinnamon sugar is made by combining ¼ cup sugar with 1 tbsp. cinnamon.

Method:
1. Core apples, but do not pare.
2. Cut each into 4 rings.
3. Melt butter* in large skillet, and place apple rings in single layer.
4. Cook slowly for 5 minutes, then turn and cook for an additional 5 minutes.
5. Sprinkle with cinnamon sugar and serve hot.

Note: Great with pork roast.

> * If you prefer a nice red color, add 3 or 4 drops of red food coloring to the melted butter.

PART II Additional Recipes

Appetizers

BEEF TERIYAKI STRIPS

2 ingredients

YIELD : 40 to 50 strips

2 lbs. filet steak
1 8-oz. bottle teriyaki marinade (I use Lawry's Teriyaki Barbecue Marinade, but you may mix ¼ cup
soy sauce with ¾ cup bottled Hawaiian Salad
Dressing.)

Method:

1. Cut meat into ½-inch-wide slices, then into shoestring strips
   approximately 3 inches x ¼ inch.
2. Marinate for several hours in the teriyaki sauce.
3. String each strip on wooden skewer, using "in-and-out" darn-
   ing motion.
4. At serving time, barbecue over hot coals on hibachi or any
   type of charcoal grill. At a party, invite each guest to cook
   his own meat to desired doneness. It takes only a minute or
   two as the strips are so thin.

These may be assembled ahead of time and refrigerated.

CHEESE BALL

4 ingredients

YIELD : 24

½ lb. bleu cheese
½ lb. cream cheese (I use Philadelphia.)
4 tbsp. French onion dip (I use Kraft's French Onion Teez Dip.)
1 cup (approx.) chopped pecans

Method:
1. Mix first 3 ingredients in a bowl.
2. Roll into a ball with your hands.
3. Pour chopped nuts into a paper bag.
4. Shake cheese ball and nuts together until cheese is well covered.
5. Refrigerate.
6. Remove from refrigerator one hour before serving. Place cheese ball on plate or serving dish. Arrange crackers around it. Place butter knife nearby and let guests serve themselves.

TOM THUMB CHEESE SNACKS

4 ingredients

YIELD : 4½ dozen

8 oz. grated Cheddar cheese
¼ lb. butter or margarine
⅓ cup sifted all-purpose flour
3 cups Kellogg's Special K cereal

Method:
1. Beat together cheese and butter until thoroughly combined.
2. Mix in flour and Special K. Drop by rounded teaspoonfuls onto ungreased baking sheet.
3. Bake in slow oven (325°) for about 20 minutes or until lightly browned around edges. Serve hot.

May be made ahead.

CHEESE SQUARES

4 ingredients

YIELD : 4 dozen

¼ lb. butter
1 egg
½ lb. Old English cheese, grated (I use Kraft.)
⅔ loaf sandwich bread (approx. 16 slices)

Method:
1. Let butter soften.
2. Beat together the egg, butter, and cheese.
3. Trim crusts from bread and spread each slice with cheese mixture, reserving some for outside frosting.
4. Cut each slice into 9 pieces (3 squares across and 3 down).
5. Put 3 squares together (one on top of another) and frost sides with mixture.
6. Just before serving, bake for about 10 minutes in preheated oven at 375°.

These may be made ahead of time and frozen. Thaw about 30 minutes at room temperature before baking.

CREAMY CLAM DIP

4 ingredients

SERVES 10 to 12

2 3-oz. pkgs. cream cheese (I use Philadelphia.)
2 cups French onion dip (or, if you prefer, commercial sour cream)
1 7½-oz. can minced clams with juice
1 7½-oz. pkg. potato chips

Method:
1. Let cream cheese stand until room temperature.
2. Mash cheese and onion dip together with fork or with electric beater.
3. Fold clams in gently.

Use as dip for potato chips.

CUCUMBER-CREAM CHEESE LOGS

4 ingredients

YIELD : 12 to 15

2 3-oz. pkgs. cream cheese (I use Philadelphia.)
2–3 cucumbers, about 6″ long
2 tbsp. milk
1 ½-oz. pkg. dill-seasoning dip mix (I use Laura Scudder.)*

* 2 tbsp. garlic-onion salad-dressing mix may be substituted (I use Schilling.)

Method:
1. Let cream cheese come to room temperature.
2. Peel cucumbers. Cut off ends. With apple corer, scoop out the soft pulp in center. Dry carefully with paper towels.
3. Stir cream cheese, milk, and dip mix until smooth.
4. Fill centers of cucumbers. Easy to do with a cake decorator tube or you may pack it in with a spoon as firmly as possible. Try to avoid air spaces.
5. Wrap each cucumber tightly in wax paper, Saran Wrap, or foil. Chill in refrigerator for several hours.
6. At serving time cut into ¾-inch slices.

Note: May be used as an appetizer, as part of an antipasto platter, or served on lettuce.

RUMAKIS

4 ingredients

YIELD : 18

6 chicken livers
1 5-oz. can water chestnuts (about 6 large ones to a can)
9 strips bacon
1 cup soy sauce

Method:
1. Cut chicken livers into thirds.
2. Cut water chestnuts into thirds.
3. Cut bacon strips in half.
4. Marinate chicken livers and water chestnuts in soy sauce for 3 or 4 hours.

5. Wrap a piece of liver around each piece of water chestnut, then cover each with a piece of bacon, stretching it a little to enclose securely. Fasten with toothpick.
6. Chill in refrigerator until ready to cook.
7. Arrange on wire rack over shallow roasting pan.
8. Bake at 400° for 20 minutes, turning occasionally.

HAWAIIAN MEATBALLS

3 ingredients

YIELD : 8

1 13¼-oz. can crushed pineapple
2 8-oz. cans meatballs in gravy (I use Chef Boy-ar-dee.)
1 tbsp. soy sauce

Method:
1. Drain pineapple.
2. Combine ingredients.
3. Keep hot in top of chafing dish.
4. Spear with toothpicks.

ONION PUFFS

4 ingredients

YIELD : 24 to 30

1 white sandwich loaf (24 to 30 slices)
4 small white onions, about 1 inch in diameter
½ cup mayonnaise
½ cup grated Parmesan cheese

Method:
1. With a biscuit cutter or sharp-edged tumbler, cut a circle from each slice of bread.
2. Cut onions into very thin slices. Place 1 slice on each bread circle.
3. Place 1 teaspoon mayonnaise on top of each.
4. Top with 1 teaspoon Parmesan cheese.
5. Broil until mayonnaise bubbles and cheese turns light brown.

Note: Onion Puffs are very popular at the cocktail hour. Allow 3 per person.

TINY PIZZAS

3 ingredients

YIELD: 20

½ lb. Mozzarella cheese
1 8-oz. tube refrigerator biscuits (I use Pillsbury.)
1 cup sandwich sauce (I use Hunt's Manwich or 1 cup bottled barbecue sauce.)

Method:
1. Cut cheese into ½-inch cubes.
2. Place halves of biscuits on cookie sheet.
3. Place a cube of cheese on top of each.
4. Cover with 1 teaspoon sandwich sauce.
5. Bake in hot oven (550°) for 5 to 8 minutes, until cheese is melted and puffy. Serve piping hot.

Note: For topping, after baking, take your choice of one of these—chopped ripe olives; chopped canned mushrooms; anchovies; chopped shrimp; sliced stuffed green olives; sliced salami.

SHRIMP PASTE FOR CRACKERS

3 ingredients

SERVES 15 to 20

1 lb. cooked shrimp
¾ cup cole slaw dressing (I use Kraft.)
Crackers (I use plain Ritz or sesame seed.)

Method:
1. Put shrimp through fine blade of food chopper.
2. Add cole slaw dressing and mix thoroughly. If necessary, add a little more dressing. Mixture should be of spreadable consistency.
3. Refrigerate.
4. Place shrimp mixture in center of serving plate. Stick small knife into mixture. Arrange crackers around the edge of plate, and let guests serve themselves.

Beverages

BLACK COW

3 ingredients

YIELD : 1

1 tbsp. milk or cream
1 12-oz. can root beer, chilled
1 scoop vanilla ice cream

Method:
1. Mix milk with about ½ cup root beer in a tall 12-oz. glass.
2. Add ice cream, then fill to top with root beer.
3. Stir gently to mix and serve immediately with straw and long spoon.

Note: This drink is equally good made with ginger ale, any cola, strawberry soda, grape juice, or whatever.

ICED RUSSIAN COFFEE

3 ingredients

SERVES 1

½ cup double-strength coffee
2 tbsp. chocolate syrup
1 large scoop vanilla ice cream

Method:
1. Place all ingredients in tall 10-oz. glass.
2. Stir vigorously.
3. Add enough ice to bring liquid up to rim of glass.

HOT MULLED CIDER

4 ingredients

YIELD: 10 cups or 20 punch cups*

4 cups pineapple juice
6 cups apple cider or apple juice
3 sticks whole cinnamon
2 tsp. whole cloves

> * For the large 30-cup coffee maker, increase amounts to:
> 3 qts. pineapple juice
> 4½ qts. apple cider
> 9 sticks whole cinnamon
> 6 tsp. whole cloves
> Yield: 30 cups or 60 punch cups

Method:

1. Pour pineapple juice and apple cider into electric coffee maker.
2. Place cinnamon sticks and whole cloves in basket of coffee maker.
3. Allow coffee maker to go through its regular cycle.

Hot mulled cider is a festive holiday beverage, particularly suitable at Christmas time. If the cider is made in an electric coffee maker, it will automatically remain at correct temperature.

DAIQUIRI

2 ingredients

SERVES 1

1½ oz. light rum
½ oz. frozen lime concentrate

Optional: twist of lime

Method:
1. Combine rum and lime concentrate in cocktail shaker with ice cubes.
2. Shake vigorously until there is frost on the shaker.
3. Strain into chilled cocktail glass. Serve plain or with twist of lime.

GRAPEFRUIT-JUICE MINT JULEP

3 ingredients

SERVES 4

1 cup fresh mint leaves without stems
½ blenderful crushed ice
3 cups grapefruit juice

Optional: fresh mint dipped into powdered sugar

Method:
1. Place ingredients into blender half filled with ice.
2. Blend together at medium speed for 1 minute or until smooth.
3. Pour into stemmed goblets.

Note: If you wish, for garnish dip a sprig of fresh mint into powdered sugar and tuck into each glass.

MAI TAIS

2 ingredients

SERVES 4

6 oz. light rum
1 fifth bottle Mai Tai mix

Method:
1. Fill Old-fashioned glasses or punch cups with crushed ice.
2. Add 1½ oz. of rum to each glass.
3. Add Mai Tai mix to top of glass and stir.

Note: As the rum and mix are poured into the glasses, the ice melts, thus reducing content. The melted ice dilutes it to just the right strength.

MANHATTAN

3 ingredients

SERVES 1

1½ oz. bourbon or rye whiskey
½ oz. sweet vermouth
1 dash Angostura bitters

Optional: Maraschino cherry or lemon twist

Method:
1. Combine ingredients in pitcher.
2. Stir with 2 ice cubes. Do not shake.
3. Pour into cocktail glass without ice.

Note: Garnish with Maraschino cherry or lemon twist, if you wish.

DRY MARTINI

2 ingredients

SERVES 1

2 oz. gin
½ oz. dry vermouth

Optional: olives, cocktail onions, or lemon twist

Method:
1. Combine ingredients in pitcher.
2. Stir with 2 ice cubes. Do not shake.
3. Pour into cocktail glass without ice.

Note: Garnish with olives, cocktail onions, or lemon twist, if you wish.

INSTANT OLD-FASHIONEDS

4 ingredients

SERVES 1

Crushed ice
2 tsp. Old-fashioned mix syrup (*see next recipe*)
1 cooked orange slice
1 Maraschino cherry
2 oz. bourbon (approx.)

Method:
1. Fill Old-fashioned glass with crushed ice.
2. Add syrup mixture.
3. Secure an orange slice and a Maraschino cherry on a toothpick and place in glass.
4. Fill glass to top with bourbon.

Note: As the syrup mixture and bourbon are poured into the glass, the ice melts, thus reducing content. The melted ice dilutes it to just the right strength.

OLD-FASHIONED MIX SYRUP

3 ingredients

YIELD : 20 portions

2 oranges
2 cups sugar, dissolved in 2 cups boiling water
1 8-oz. bottle Maraschino cherries

Method:
1. Cut oranges into 5 slices, then cut each slice in half.
2. Cook together for 5 minutes the orange slices, sugar, and water.
3. Pour into quart jar. Add drained Maraschino cherries. (This is for convenience so that all will be in one jar.)
4. Store in refrigerator until ready to use.

See preceding recipe for directions for using this mix.

Breads
and Sandwiches

BACON BARS

4 ingredients

YIELD: 18

6 slices bacon
½ cup shredded sharp Cheddar cheese
2 cups packaged biscuit mix (I use Bisquick.)
3 tbsp. bacon fat

Method:
1. Cook bacon until crisp, then crumble into small pieces. Reserve bacon fat.
2. Stir cheese and bacon into dry biscuit mix. Make dough according to directions on package, but use bacon fat instead of salad oil.
3. Knead as directed for rolled biscuits. Roll dough out to measure 6 x 10 inches. Cut into six 10-inch strips, each 1 inch wide. Cut each strip into thirds crosswise.
4. Place the bars 1 inch apart on cookie sheet. Bake at 450° for 10 minutes or until nicely browned.

Note: May be prepared in advance, placed on cookie sheet, and refrigerated until time to bake. Bake 5 minutes extra.

CHEESE DREAMS

3 ingredients

YIELD: 4

4 slices bacon
4 slices white bread
4 slices medium-sharp Cheddar cheese

Optional: tomato slices

Method:
1. Fry bacon slightly.
2. Toast one side of bread slices.
3. Lay slice of cheese on untoasted side.*
4. Lay piece of bacon on top of cheese.
5. Broil until cheese melts and bacon browns a little. Watch closely for they burn easily. Serve hot.

---

* Tomato slices are good too, and should be placed between cheese and bacon.

SAUTÉED MARMALADE STRIPS

3 ingredients

SERVES 1

2 slices white bread
2 tbsp. marmalade (Any thick jam such as strawberry or peach may be used.)
2 tbsp. butter or margarine

Method:
1. Make orange-marmalade sandwich, omitting butter.
2. Cut off the crusts.
3. Fry sandwich slowly in butter until brown, then turn and fry other side.
4. Cut into three strips. Serve hot.

EASY EASY MUFFINS

4 ingredients

YIELD: 12

2 cups self-rising flour
1 cup buttermilk
¼ cup mayonnaise
¼ cup sugar

Method:
1. Combine ingredients and blend. Batter will be slightly lumpy.
2. Fill greased cups of muffin tins two-thirds full.
3. Bake at 375° for 18 minutes or until light golden brown.

ONION-BACON CRUNCH BREAD OR ROLLS

3 ingredients

YIELD: 12 to 16

¼ lb. butter or margarine
4 tbsp. imitation crumbled bacon with minced onion pieces (I use Lawry's Baconion.)
1 loaf Brown 'n Serve bread slices or 1 pkg. Brown 'n Serve Rolls

Method:
1. Melt butter.
2. Mix Baconion with melted butter. Spread over top of bread or rolls.
3. Bake according to directions on package.

ORANGE BLOSSOM ROLLS

3 ingredients

YIELD : 12

    1 8-oz. tube refrigerator rolls (I use Pillsbury's Butterflake Dinner Rolls.)
    1 orange
    1 to 1½ cups confectioners' sugar

Method:
1. Bake rolls according to directions on package.
2. Grate orange to obtain 1 tbsp. of rind.
3. Squeeze juice from orange. Add rind.
4. Add confectioners' sugar to orange juice until you have a fairly stiff frosting.
5. When rolls are baked, frost them and serve hot. If you wish, you can slash rolls with sharp knife and put frosting inside too.

May be baked several hours ahead, then reheated.

FRENCH DIP ROLLS

3 ingredients

SERVES 2

    2 medium-sized hard French rolls
    1 10½-oz. can beef broth or consommé
    4 slices leftover roast beef

Method:
1. Warm rolls.
2. Heat broth to boiling point.
3. Slice roast beef thin.
4. Cut each roll in two lengthwise. Place two slices of beef on bottom half of each, then replace "lids."
5. Set each roll on dinner-size plate and place a cupful of hot broth on same plate.
6. Serve at once. (Guest dips roll into hot broth before each bite.)

Note: This is one of the most delicious ways of using up left-over roast.

RASPBERRY JELLY ROLLS

3 ingredients

YIELD: 12

3 tbsp. butter or margarine
12 slices sandwich bread, very fresh
6 tbsp. raspberry jelly or jam

Method:
1. Allow butter to soften.
2. With sharp knife, cut crusts from bread.
3. Spread slices with butter, then with jelly.
4. Roll each slice as for jelly roll and secure each one with a toothpick.
5. Place on shallow baking sheet and brown under broiler, turning once; or brown lightly in hot oven (400°).

MINCED-CHICKEN SANDWICHES ALMONDINE

4 ingredients

YIELD: approx. 24 open-faced sandwiches

½ cup slivered almonds
1 loaf white sandwich bread
2 cups minced chicken
½ cup boiled salad dressing or bottled cole slaw dressing (I use Kraft.)

Method:
1. Pour almonds into pie tin and bake in 350° oven for 15–20 minutes or until toasted a light brown.
2. With a biscuit cutter or sharp-edged tumbler, cut a circle from each slice of bread.
3. Combine chicken and dressing. If necessary, add more dressing to make of spreadable consistency.
4. Spread on bread circles.
5. Sprinkle toasted nuts on top.

Note: When planning to serve these at parties, make several hours in advance and arrange on serving plate or platter. Wrap all securely in Saran Wrap to keep fresh. Refrigerate until ready to serve.

MYSTERY GOURMET SANDWICH

4 ingredients

<small>YIELD</small> : 2

    2 slices bacon
    ½ cup chopped walnuts
    2 tbsp. mayonnaise
    4 slices white or wheat bread

Method:
1. Cook bacon until crisp, then crumble.
2. Combine with chopped walnuts and enough mayonnaise to moisten.
3. Use as filling between two slices of bread.
4. Trim crusts if desired.

Desserts

ANGEL FOOD CAKE WITH
RASPBERRIES AND WHIPPED CREAM

3 ingredients

SERVES 4

1 16-oz. angel food cake from bakery
2 pkgs. frozen raspberries
1 9-oz. carton frozen whipped cream (I use Cool Whip.)

Method:
1. Tear angel cake into serving pieces and place in a large bowl with tongs for serving.
2. Partly thaw raspberries and place in a small serving bowl.
3. Place whipped cream in a third bowl.
4. Pass bowl of cake pieces to guests, who serve themselves. Then pass raspberries, followed by bowl of whipped cream.

May be assembled ahead.

Note: If you prefer, the dessert can be placed on plates in kitchen at the last minute and brought to table.

APPLE SNOW PUDDING

4 ingredients

SERVES 4

1 ¼-oz. envelope unflavored gelatin (I use Knox.)
1 cup unsweetened applesauce
2 egg whites
⅔ cup sugar

Optional: cinnamon

Method:
1. Soften gelatin in 1 tablespoon cold water.
2. Heat applesauce to just under the boil.
3. Add gelatin and stir until blended. Chill in refrigerator until partially set, then beat until frothy.
4. Beat egg whites until stiff. Add sugar a little at a time, beating after each addition. Fold into cooled applesauce-gelatin mixture.
5. Spoon into sherbet glasses and, if you wish, sprinkle with a little cinnamon.
6. Chill in refrigerator for several hours or overnight.

APPLE TURNOVERS

2 ingredients

YIELD: 6 to 8

1 9¼-oz. pkg. piecrust sticks (I use Pillsbury.)
1 21-oz. can apple pie filling (In place of apples, you may use peach, blueberry, or pumpkin pie filling.)

Method:
1. Prepare piecrust as directed on package.
2. Grease cups of muffin tins, 2½ to 3 inches in diameter.
3. Roll pastry to ⅛-inch thickness on lightly floured board and cut into 4-inch squares. Lay squares in cups of muffin tin.
4. Spoon in 2 or 3 tablespoons of filling. Fold pastry corners together over the mixture.
5. Bake for 10 minutes at 450°, then for 30 minutes at 350°.

APRICOT CRISP

4 ingredients

SERVES 4 to 6

1 17-oz. can apricot halves, drained
⅛ lb. butter (4 tbsp.)
½ cup brown sugar
½ cup flour

Optional: whipped cream or ice cream

Method:
1. Place apricots in bottom of 1-quart buttered casserole.*
2. Crumb together butter, brown sugar, and flour.
3. Spread over apricots.
4. Bake for 45 minutes at 350°, or until crumbs are golden brown. Serve warm. Top with whipped cream or ice cream if desired.

 * A 9 x 13-inch glass baking dish works well when doubling this recipe.

BAKED ALASKA DESSERT

4 ingredients

SERVES 6 to 8

16-oz. bakery sponge cake
1 qt. ice cream
2 egg whites
4 tbsp. powdered sugar

Method:
1. Cut sponge cake into 2 layers. Store in freezer compartment until ready to assemble.
2. Place one layer of sponge cake in an 8-inch-square cake pan and cover with thick, even layer of firm ice cream; top with second layer of cake.
3. Cover top and sides with thick layer of meringue made by beating egg whites stiff and beating sugar into them. Return to freezer until serving time.
4. Put the dessert into the oven preheated to 500° and bake about 3 minutes or until lightly browned.
5. Immediately slip dessert onto a chilled plate and serve at the table.

Note: For special occasions, try dipping 6 to 8 sugar cubes in lemon extract; then place the cubes on top of dessert just before serving. Light the cubes and bring to table flaming.

BAKED BANANAS

3 ingredients

SERVES 4

4 firm bananas
1½ tbsp. butter or margarine
¾ cup cranberry sauce

Method:
1. Peel bananas. Place, whole, in well-greased, oven-to-table baking dish.
2. Melt butter.
3. Brush bananas well with butter.
4. Bake in 375° oven for 15–18 minutes until bananas are soft.
5. Serve with hot cranberry sauce poured over bananas.

Note: May be served as meat accompaniment or as dessert.

BANANA-COCONUT CREAM PIE

4 ingredients

SERVES 6

2 3-oz. pkgs. vanilla pudding
1 ready-to-bake pie shell from frozen-food section of market or make your own. *See pages 100–101.*
2 bananas
½ cup grated coconut

Method:
1. Make pudding according to directions on package.
2. Bake pie shell and allow to cool.
3. Slice bananas into baked pie shell.
4. Pour cooled pudding over bananas.
5. Sprinkle grated coconut over pudding.
6. Brown 5–10 minutes in 400° oven to lightly toast coconut. Watch carefully, as it burns easily.

May be made a day in advance and refrigerated until time to serve.

QUICK BISCUIT TORTONI

4 ingredients

SERVES 4

1 pt. vanilla ice cream
8 Maraschino cherries
12 salted almonds
⅓ cup macaroon crumbs

Method:
1. Take ice cream out of refrigerator to soften for 10–15 minutes while you prepare other ingredients.
2. Chop cherries and almonds very fine.
3. Mix with ice cream in a bowl, using your hands as if you were making bread.
4. Fill 4 parfait or sherbet glasses.
5. Sprinkle with macaroon crumbs.
6. Cover tops with aluminum foil, then set in freezer. (No, the glasses won't break.) Remove from freezer 10 minutes before serving.

Note: These may be made in paper cups.

JIFFY BOSTON CREAM PIE

3 ingredients

SERVES 6

1 9-oz. pkg. white cake mix
2 cups ready-to-eat vanilla pudding (I use Betty Crocker.)
2 tbsp. confectioners' sugar

Method:
1. Mix cake according to directions on package. Pour into greased 8- or 9-inch-round cake pan. Bake and cool.
2. Split cake horizontally with sharp knife to make two round layers.
3. Spread vanilla pudding between layers.
4. Sprinkle top of cake with confectioners' sugar.

May be made several hours in advance, then refrigerated. May be served chilled or at room temperature.

BRAZIL-NUT ICE CREAM TORTE

4 ingredients

SERVES 8

1½ cups Brazil nuts
1 egg white
¼ cup sugar
1½ qts. vanilla ice cream

Method:
1. Set oven at 300°.
2. Grind Brazil nuts with medium blade in food grinder. Reserve ¼ cup chopped nuts to decorate top.
3. Beat together egg white and sugar until foamy, then stir in ground nuts. Beat until stiff but not dry.
4. Spread mixture into well-greased, 8-inch-square cake pan.
5. Reduce heat to 250° and bake in slow oven for 60 minutes. Cool.
6. Spread on top slightly softened ice cream.
7. Decorate by sprinkling the remaining ¼ cup chopped nuts around outer edge of torte.
8. Place in freezer until 10 minutes before serving time. Cut in serving pieces approximately 2 inches by 4 inches.

CHERRIES JUBILEE ALMONDINE

4 ingredients

SERVES 4

> 1 17-oz. can Bing cherries, the pitted, sweet, dark-red variety (I use Del Monte.)
> 1 3-oz. pkg. cherry gelatin
> ¼ cup slivered almonds
> 1 cup whipped cream or sour cream

Method:
1. Drain the cherries and set aside, saving juice.
2. Use the canned cherry juice and add enough water to make 1½ cups.
3. Heat and pour over gelatin. Stir until gelatin dissolves.
4. Add almonds and cherries. Refrigerate for several hours or overnight.
5. Break up gently with fork, and spoon into sherbet glasses.
6. Top with whipped cream or sour cream.

CHOCOLATE-CHIP INDIVIDUAL TORTES

2 ingredients

SERVES 4

> 1 16-oz. tube refrigerator chocolate-chip cookies (I use Pillsbury.)
> 1 5-oz. can ready-to-eat vanilla pudding (I use Del Monte.)

Method:
1. Make cookies according to directions on package. Do *not* over-bake.
2. When cool, using 3 to a stack, spread vanilla pudding between layers and on top, spreading to edge so that part will flow down to cover sides. Arrange on serving plate.
3. Chill for several hours so that ingredients blend together.

CHOCOLATE-CHIP TART SHELLS

2 ingredients

YIELD : 20

1 16-oz. tube refrigerater chocolate-chip cookies
Soft butter (enough to grease cups of small, 1½-inch muffin tin and to coat hands for easier handling of dough)

Method:
1. Grease cups of muffin tin with butter.
2. Remove cookie dough from refrigerator, and while still cold slice it ¼-inch thick. Butter your hands and roll each slice of dough into a ball. When dough gets a trifle soft, press evenly on bottom and sides of cups in muffin tin.
3. Follow directions on package for baking. You'll notice that the bottoms puff up a little, but there is still room for a filling. Tarts look especially inviting when filling is piled up in the center.

Note: The tart shells may be filled with prepared vanilla pudding, whipped cream, ice cream, or applesauce.

SURPRISE CHOCOLATE COOKIES

3 ingredients

YIELD : 16

1 tube refrigerator sugar cookies (I use Pillsbury.)
1 10-oz. pkg. *solid* chocolate mints or chocolate candies (I use Hershey's Milk Chocolate Kisses.)
½ cup chopped walnuts

Method:
1. Cut chilled cookie dough in ½-inch slices.
2. With buttered hands roll each slice into a ball.
3. Push a piece of chocolate candy into center of each, then roll into smooth ball again so that cookie dough completely encloses the piece of candy.
4. Arrange on greased cookie sheet 2 inches apart. Sprinkle with chopped nuts.
5. Refrigerate for 1 hour or more.
6. Bake for 15–18 minutes in 375° oven until light brown.
7. Cool for 5 minutes before removing from cookie sheet.

CHOCOLATE CREAM CHEESECAKE

4 ingredients

SERVES 6 to 8

1 8-oz. pkg. cream cheese (I use Philadelphia.)
1 6.5-oz. pkg. graham-cracker-crust mix (I use Betty Crocker, which requires no mixing.)
1½ cups half and half cream (Available in the dairy section of your market.)
2 5-oz. cans ready-to-eat chocolate fudge pudding (I use Del Monte.)

Optional: For a richer dessert, top with sour cream or whipped cream.

Method:
1. Soften cream cheese by bringing it to room temperature.
2. Empty crust mix into 8- or 9-inch pie plate, and press firmly and evenly against sides and bottom of pan with back of spoon or with your fingers. Bake according to directions.
3. In a bowl, with rotary beater, blend together the cream cheese and ½ cup of half and half.
4. Add remaining half and half and then the pudding. Beat until just blended, 1 to 2 minutes.
5. Pour into cooled crust. Refrigerate.

CHOCOLATE MINT PUDDING

4 ingredients

SERVES 4

1 3-oz. pkg. vanilla pudding mix
2 cups milk
15 chocolate peppermints
1½ tbsp. butter

Method:
1. Prepare pudding as directed and pour into 4 dessert glasses. Chill.
2. At serving time, put the chocolate peppermints and the butter in top of double boiler and place over hot water. Stir until peppermints are completely melted. Cool slightly and pour over pudding.

Note: This sauce is also good over ice cream or angel food cake.

CHOCOLATE PUFFS

4 ingredients

YIELD: 30

2 egg whites
2 cups confectioners' sugar
2 squares semisweet chocolate
2 tbsp. cornstarch

Method:
1. Beat egg whites until very stiff.
2. Add sugar gradually, beating after each addition.
3. Grate chocolate and mix with cornstarch.
4. Beat into egg-white mixture.
5. Drop slightly rounded teaspoonfuls on greased cookie sheet 2 inches apart.
6. Bake at 300° for 25–30 minutes or until light brown in color.

Note: These light-as-air cookies are low in calories—about 50 each.

COCONUT MACAROONS

4 ingredients

YIELD: 2½ dozen

3 egg whites
1 cup sugar
3 cups shredded coconut
2 tbsp. cornstarch

Optional: 1 tsp. vanilla extract

Method:
1. Beat egg whites until very stiff.
2. Slowly add sugar, beating after each addition. Add vanilla if desired.
3. With spoon, fold in coconut mixed with cornstarch.
4. Drop by teaspoonfuls 1 inch apart on greased cookie sheet.
5. Bake for 20–25 minutes, until light brown.

TOASTED-COCONUT PIE

3 ingredients

SERVES 6

2 cups shredded coconut (Especially delicious made with fresh coconut.)
2 tbsp. softened butter or margarine
1 qt. vanilla ice cream

Method:
1. To toast coconut, pour desired amount into pie tin and place in 300° oven for 8–10 minutes, stirring once or twice. Remove when coconut becomes light brown.
2. Spread softened butter evenly into sides and bottom of 8- or 9-inch pie plate.
3. Pat 1½ cups of the toasted coconut into the butter, on sides as well as bottom.
4. Bake at 300° for 15–20 minutes until golden brown. Cool.
5. Remove ice cream from freezer and allow to soften for 10–15 minutes.
6. Fill pie shell with ice cream; then sprinkle with remaining ½ cup of toasted coconut.
7. Place in freezer. Remove 15 minutes before serving time.

CONFETTI SNOWBALL FREEZE

4 ingredients

SERVES 8 to 10

1 doz. (approx.) coconut macaroons from bakery
2 qts. vanilla ice cream
1 pt. raspberry sherbet
1 pt. lime sherbet

Method:
1. Line bottom of angel-cake pan (or large gelatin mold) with wax paper. Chill pan.
2. Crumble macaroons to make about 3 cupfuls of crumbs. Sprinkle a layer of crumbs on bottom of pan.
3. Arrange a layer of ice-cream balls and sherbet balls (well mixed as to color) on top of crumbs. Fill in spaces with crumbs.
4. Repeat layers until pan is filled solidly.
5. Freeze overnight. Unmold on chilled serving plate and serve at table. With a sharp knife, cut straight down through the layers and serve wedge-shaped pieces.

CRÈME DE MENTHE-CHOCOLATE DESSERT

4 ingredients

SERVES 8

1 pt. heavy cream
1 box cream-filled chocolate cookies (I use Oreo.)
1 7-oz. jar marshmallow crème
⅓ cup crème de menthe liqueur

Method:
1. Whip cream.
2. Crush Oreo cookies into crumbs. Arrange half of them in bottom of pie plate.
3. Mix together the marshmallow crème and crème de menthe.
4. Fold in whipped cream.
5. Pour over the crumbs.
6. Top with remaining cookie crumbs.
7. Freeze. Remove from freezer 5 minutes before serving. Cut in pie-shaped pieces.

CUSTARD CRÈME BRULÉE

3 ingredients

SERVES 4

½ cup sugar
3 cups milk
1 4½-oz. pkg. custard mix (I use Jell-O Golden Egg Custard.)

Method:
1. Heat oven to 400°.
2. Pour sugar into 1-quart casserole and place in 400° oven. When sugar melts and turns light brown, approximately 15 minutes, remove from oven and roll casserole quickly to partially coat sides.
3. Add milk to custard mix in a saucepan and cook according to directions on package.
4. Pour hot custard over caramelized sugar. Cool, then refrigerate for 4 or 5 hours or overnight.
5. Unmold on serving dish.

NEVER-FAIL CUT-OUT COOKIES

4 ingredients

YIELD: 18

½ cup sugar
½ lb. butter or margarine
1 egg
3 cups self-rising flour

Method:
1. Beat together the sugar, softened butter, and egg. (I use an electric beater.)
2. Add flour gradually until well blended, then knead for a few minutes as if you were making piecrust.
3. Roll small amounts of dough, ¼-inch thick, on a lightly floured board. Cut with cookie cutters.
4. Bake on ungreased cookie sheet 10–12 minutes at 350°. They should be light brown in color.
5. Frost as desired. (For frosting suggestions, see next recipe.)

Note: This recipe makes 8 wonderful tart shells. For Lemon-Honey Filling, *see page 95.*

FROSTINGS

3 ingredients

YIELD: 1 cup

2 cups confectioners' sugar
Food coloring
Flavor extracts

Method:
1. Sift confectioners' sugar into large bowl.
2. Add hot water (approximately 3–4 tablespoons) *very slowly* to the sugar until you have a frosting just thin enough to spread.
3. To make a pretty and flavorful assortment, divide frosting among four small bowls, and use a different combination of food coloring and flavoring for each bowl. The following combinations are recommended:

Food coloring	*Flavor extract*
Yellow	Lemon
Orange	Orange
Green	Peppermint
Pink	Rose (usually available in pharmacies)
Blue	Almond
White	Vanilla

FORTUNE KISSES

4 ingredients

YIELD: 16

1 egg white
1 cup dark brown sugar, firmly packed
½ tsp. vanilla
½ cup chopped pecans

Method:
1. Beat egg white until stiff, but not dry.
2. Add brown sugar. Beat very stiff until light in color.
3. Add vanilla and fold in pecans.
4. Drop from a teaspoon on lightly greased baking sheet.
5. Bake for 15 minutes at 300°.

Note: For party fare, type fortunes on thin paper, roll into tiny cylinders, and insert in each mound of dough after dropping from teaspoon.

WARM GINGERBREAD WITH WHIPPED CREAM AND CANDIED GINGER

3 ingredients

SERVES 6

1 14-oz. pkg. gingerbread mix (I use Betty Crocker.)
5 or 6 pieces candied ginger
1 9-oz. carton prepared whipped cream (found in frozen-food section of market. I use Cool Whip.)

Method:
1. Prepare and bake gingerbread mix according to directions on package.
2. If made in advance, place in oven a few minutes to warm up again just before serving.
3. Cut candied ginger into very thin strips.
4. Place a tablespoon or two of whipped cream on top of each serving, then poke in a few strips of candied ginger.

LEMON-CHEESE PIE

4 ingredients

SERVES 6

    1 6.5-oz. pkg. graham-cracker crust (I use Betty Crocker.)
    1 8-oz. pkg. cream cheese (I use Philadelphia.)
1½ cups milk
    1 3¼-oz. pkg. lemon instant pudding (I use Jell-O.)

    Optional: 2 tbsp. grated lemon peel

Method:
1. Prepare crust according to directions on package.
2. Let cream cheese stand in medium bowl till room temperature, then add ½ cup milk and mix cheese and milk together until smooth. Add grated lemon peel, if desired.
3. Add remaining milk and pudding mix, beating slowly with rotary beater just until blended, about 1–2 minutes.
4. Pour into prepared crust. Chill in refrigerator at least 1 hour.

LEMON-CREAM TARTS

4 ingredients

YIELD: 8

1 cup frozen lemonade concentrate
1 pkg. tart shells (Available either unbaked in frozen-food department or ready-baked in the cake-mix department. Either way, shells come 8 to a package, each tart in its own aluminum foil tin.)
6 eggs
2 5-oz. cans ready-to-eat vanilla pudding (I use Del Monte.)

Method:
1. Defrost lemonade concentrate.
2. Bake tart shells according to directions on package (if using the unbaked variety).
3. Beat eggs well, preferably with electric beater.
4. Add lemonade concentrate and continue beating until blended.
5. Cook in top of double boiler until thickened, stirring constantly. Remove from heat and set aside to cool.
6. Blend in the vanilla pudding, then fill baked tart shells.

LEMON-HONEY FILLING

4 ingredients

YIELD : fills 6 to 8 tarts

6 eggs
2 heaping tbsp. butter
1 cup sugar
2 medium lemons, juice and grated rind (rind not to exceed 2 tbsp.)

Method:
1. Beat eggs well.
2. Add remaining ingredients. Continue to beat well.
3. Place mixture in double boiler and cook until thick, stirring constantly.
4. Chill before using.

Note: My favorite way of using it is as a filling for tarts made of Never-Fail cookie dough, *see page 91.* It is also a delicious filling for a graham-cracker pie crust or for a layer cake.

MINCEMEAT SQUARES

4 ingredients

YIELD : 24

2 cups graham-cracker crumbs
1⅓ cups mincemeat (I use Borden's None Such.)
1 14-oz. can condensed—not evaporated—milk (I use Borden's Eagle Brand Sweetened Condensed Milk.)
½ cup chopped nuts

Optional: powdered sugar

Method:
1. Mix all ingredients together in a large bowl.
2. Spoon into well-greased 9 x 13 x 2-inch baking dish.
3. Bake in preheated 350° oven for about 35–40 minutes or until lightly browned.
4. Cool in pan before cutting.

Before serving, shake squares in bag with powdered sugar, if desired.

Note: These travel exceptionally well.

NUT MACAROON WAFERS

4 ingredients

YIELD : 18

2 egg whites
½ cup sugar
½ tsp. almond extract
½ cup ground almonds

Method:
1. Preheat oven at 350°.
2. Beat egg whites until dry and stiff enough to hold shape.
3. Fold in sugar.
4. Add almond extract and ground almonds.
5. Drop by teaspoonfuls onto ungreased baking sheet.
6. Bake for 15–20 minutes and remove from pans at once.

NO-BAKE ORANGE BALLS

4 ingredients

YIELD: 3 dozen

½ cup frozen-orange-juice concentrate
1 7¼-oz. box vanilla wafers (I use Nabisco's "Nillas.")
¾ cup grated coconut
1½ cups confectioners' sugar

Method:
1. Thaw concentrated orange juice. Do not dilute.
2. Crush wafers into fine crumbs.
3. Mix crumbs, coconut, and ¾ cup sugar. Stir in orange juice.
4. Form mixture into 1-inch balls and roll in remaining ¾ cup confectioners' sugar.
5. Store cookie balls in tightly covered container at room temperature.

ORANGE CRÈME

4 ingredients

SERVES 6

6 small or medium-sized oranges (Choose un-
blemished thick-skinned firm oranges.)
1 cup heavy cream
¼ cup Cointreau
1 24-oz. jar orange marmalade

Method:
1. Wash oranges well. Polish. Slice small section from bottom so
   that each will stand upright on dessert plate. Slice off top, remove all pulp, and discard, leaving shells only.
2. Whip cream, add Cointreau, then fold in marmalade.
3. Spoon lightly into orange shells. Store in refrigerator to chill
   until time to serve.

May be made in advance.

Note: Nice served with crisp cookies.

ICE CREAM PARFAITS

2 ingredients

SERVES 4

1 qt. vanilla ice cream
½ cup liqueur (There are many variations of parfaits.
You may use crème de menthe, crème de cacao,
apricot or peach brandy, etc.)

Optional: 1 cup frozen raspberries, strawberries,
or peaches, in place of liqueur

Method:
1. Remove ice cream from freezer about 20 minutes before assembling parfaits.
2. Pour 2 tablespoons liqueur or fruits into each of 4 parfait glasses.*
3. Spoon ice cream into glasses, pressing down so that liqueur will be forced to the top, creating a pretty ribbon effect.
4. Cover tops of glasses with foil to protect edges. Place in freezer.
5. Remove from freezer 10 minutes before serving so that parfaits will soften somewhat.

* Parfait glasses are available in the majority of department stores. In case you are not familiar with them, they are tall, narrow ones similar to pilsener glasses.

GOLDEN PEACH TEASERS

4 ingredients

SERVES 6

1 13-oz. can peach halves, drained
⅓ cup orange liqueur (Triple Sec, Cointreau, or Curaçao)
½ cup miniature marshmallows
½ cup shredded coconut

Method:
1. Place drained peach halves cut side up in baking dish.
2. Pour liqueur around peaches, then top with marshmallows.
3. Sprinkle tops with coconut.
4. Bake at 350° for 15 minutes.

DANISH PEANUT CAKES

4 ingredients

YIELD: 4 dozen

1 pound cake from the bakery
1 16-oz. box confectioners' sugar
1 tsp. vanilla flavoring
1 lb. finely chopped peanuts (approx. 2 cups)

Method:
1. Freeze cake for several hours for easier handling.
2. Mix confectioners' sugar, flavoring, and enough hot water (try 2–3 tbsp. as a starter) to make a thin icing.
3. Cut cake into pieces approximately 1 x 1 x 1 inch.
4. Frost them one at a time by covering all sides with icing, then shake coated pieces in paper bag containing chopped peanuts. Place on cake plate leaving spaces in between so that they can dry properly.

Note: These are absolutely delicious and improve with standing.

PIE SHELL (NO ROLL)

4 ingredients

YIELD: 1 shell

½ cup vegetable oil (I use Wesson.)
2 tbsp. cold milk
2 tbsp. sugar
1½ cups flour

Method:
1. Beat oil, milk, and sugar together.
2. Pour flour into bowl and add mixture. Stir until blended.
3. Press dough evenly onto bottom and sides of 9-inch pan with fingers. Prick with fork.
4. Bake for 15–20 minutes at 375° until golden brown. Cool before filling.

Note: Here are some suggestions for fillings: fruit pie fillings such as apple, peach, blueberry, pumpkin, etc., or ready-to-eat puddings such as chocolate, butterscotch, or vanilla (I use Betty Crocker.)

PUMPKIN PARFAIT PIE

3 ingredients

SERVES 6

1 9-in. unbaked pie shell from frozen-food section at market
1 qt. vanilla ice cream
1 21-oz. can pumpkin pie filling

Optional: ½ cup candied-ginger strips

Method:
1. Bake pie shell.
2. Remove ice cream from refrigerator and allow to soften for 10–15 minutes.
3. Combine pie filling and ice cream.
4. Fill pie shell and arrange candied ginger strips on top, if desired. Enclose in plastic bag.
5. Freeze.
6. Remove from freezer 15–20 minutes before serving.

Note: Also good in a graham-cracker crust.

PINEAPPLE MOUSSE

4 ingredients

SERVES 2

    1 6-oz. can frozen-pineapple-juice concentrate
    1 lemon, juice only
    1 cup heavy cream
    ¼ cup toasted shredded coconut*

> * *To toast coconut*—Pour desired amount into pie tin and place in 300° oven for 8–10 minutes, stirring once or twice. Remove when coconut becomes light brown.

Method:
1. In a bowl, mix together pineapple and lemon juices.
2. Whip cream until it holds a point, then combine with fruit juices.
3. Pour into deep refrigerator tray and freeze until edges begin to harden. Transfer to a bowl and beat vigorously, preferably with an electric beater.
4. Return to refrigerator and freeze until almost firm. Serve in sherbet glasses with a sprinkling of toasted coconut on top.

WARM RASPBERRY COTTAGE PUDDING

4 ingredients

SERVES 8 to 10

    2 cups fresh raspberries
    1 pound cake from the bakery
    ½ cup confectioners' sugar
    1 tbsp. butter

    Optional: whipped cream or sour cream

Method:
1. Wash raspberries.
2. Cut pound cake into ¾-inch slices, allowing one slice per person. Warm slices in top section of double boiler or in covered baking dish in 200° oven.
3. Heat raspberries and sugar to boiling, stirring all the while. Remove from heat and skim any foam from top. Add butter.
4. Serve warm over warm cake slices, either plain or with a scoop of whipped cream or sour cream.

FRESH-STRAWBERRY PIE

4 ingredients

SERVES 6

4 cups whole strawberries
1 cup sugar
2 rounded tbsp. cornstarch
1 9-in. baked pie shell (available in frozen-food section of market)

Optional: whipped cream

Method:
1. Wash strawberries. Remove stems.
2. Mix sugar and cornstarch with a cup of water in a small saucepan and bring to boil.
3. Cook until clear and thick, stirring constantly. Cool slightly. For a beautiful color, add a drop or two of red coloring.
4. Stir in the whole strawberries and pour all into the baked pie shell. Refrigerate for 3–4 hours.

Top with whipped cream, if desired.

STRAWBERRY SHORTCAKE

4 ingredients

SERVES 4

2 pkgs. frozen strawberries
1 tube refrigerated buttermilk biscuits (I use Pillsbury.)
⅛ lb. butter
1 pt. half and half cream

Method:
1. Defrost strawberries.
2. Bake biscuits until medium brown on top.
3. When biscuits are done, split in half and place bottom halves on individual dessert plates. Butter them. Spoon half of the strawberries over them.
4. Cover with top halves of biscuits. Place remaining strawberries on top.
5. Serve while biscuits are still hot. Pass with pitcher of half and half.

HONEY-ALMOND SUNDAE

3 ingredients

SERVES 4

1 cup honey (liquid type)
1 qt. vanilla ice cream
4 tbsp. slivered almonds

Method:
1. Heat the honey.
2. Place ice cream in each sherbet dish.
3. Pour ¼ cup honey over each, then top with 1 tablespoon almonds.

SOUTHERN TIPSY CAKE

4 ingredients

SERVES 10 to 12

1 16-oz. angel food cake from bakery
1 cup sherry (rum, apricot or peach brandy may be used.)
1 16-oz. can ready-to-eat vanilla pudding (I use Betty Crocker.)
1 cup heavy cream

Optional: 1 cup toasted whole almonds

Method:
1. Line a bowl with Saran Wrap, allowing it to extend 3 or 4 inches over rim.
2. Break angel food cake into pieces about 1 inch in diameter, and place in bowl.
3. Stir sherry into pudding, pour over cake pieces, and toss lightly.
4. Cover and let stand several hours or overnight in refrigerator.
5. Two or three hours before serving, whip the cream.
6. Lift cake out of bowl by grasping edges of Saran Wrap and place on cake plate round side up.
7. Smother with whipped cream, and if you like, stick almonds into whipped cream all around to decorate.
8. Refrigerate until ready to serve. Cut into portions with sharp knife.

ICE-CREAM-CONE CUP CAKES
with chocolate mint topping

4 ingredients

YIELD : 12

1 box (12) flat-bottomed ice cream cones
1 9-oz. box white cake mix
½ cup chopped walnuts
½ box miniature chocolate covered mint patties (I use Nabisco's Junior Mints.)

Method:
1. Set ice cream cones in the 12 compartments of muffin tin.
2. Prepare cake mix according to directions on package, then beat in chopped nuts.
3. Half fill each cone with cake batter.
4. Bake cup cakes 25–30 minutes until slightly brown on top.
5. Remove from oven and while still hot, place 3 or 4 mint patties on top of each. They will melt and run down inside cone.

Note: These are especially nice to serve at picnics and other informal occasions, as they are eaten out of hand. These are ever so much easier to handle than those baked in paper-lined cups. They are also available in a rainbow collection, especially festive for children's parties.

Eggs and Casseroles

CORNED-BEEF-AND-CABBAGE CASSEROLE

4 ingredients

SERVES 3 to 4

1 10½-oz. can condensed cream-of-celery soup (I use Campbell.)
½ cup chopped onion
1 cup diced cooked corned beef
4 cups coarsely shredded cabbage

Optional: 1 tsp. dry mustard

Method:
1. Mix all ingredients in 1½-quart greased casserole. Cover.
2. Bake at 375° for 45 minutes.

CHICKEN-BREAST CASSEROLE

4 ingredients

SERVES 4

4 chicken breasts, cut in half to make a total of 8 pieces
¾ stick margarine
½ 1½-oz. pkg. onion-soup mix (I use Lipton.)
1 3-oz. can small button mushrooms

Method:
1. Place chicken breasts in baking dish.
2. Dice margarine and place under and over the chicken.
3. Shake onion-soup-mix package so that contents are well mixed, then sprinkle ½ package over chicken.
4. Bake at 400° for 15 minutes, then at 350° for 45 minutes.
5. Arrange mushrooms over top and continue baking for another 15 minutes.

Note: For a milder taste, shake chicken in a bag of Shake 'N Bake instead of using onion-soup mix. May be made ahead and refrigerated. Reheat for 30 minutes at 350° until bubbly.

CHICKEN OR TURKEY DIVAN

4 ingredients

SERVES 2 to 3

1 pkg. frozen broccoli spears
4 to 6 slices leftover white meat of chicken or turkey
1 10½-oz. can condensed cream-of-chicken soup
½ cup grated Parmesan cheese

Method:
1. Cook broccoli according to directions on package.
2. Arrange broccoli spears on bottom of greased casserole.
3. Place chicken slices on top of broccoli.
4. Dilute chicken soup with ½ can water. Pour over chicken.
5. Sprinkle Parmesan cheese over all.
6. Bake for 30 minutes at 300° until heated through and bubbly. Place under broiler for a minute or two to brown cheese.

Warning: Watch every second so that cheese doesn't burn.

Serve at once.

CHILI-MAC BAKE

3 ingredients

SERVES 4 to 6

1 8-oz. pkg. elbow macaroni
1 10-oz. pkg. Cheddar cheese (I use Kraft's Cracker
 Barrel, extra sharp.)
1 16-oz. can chili *without* beans

Method:

1. Bring 4 quarts salted water to a rapid boil, then add macaroni. Bring to a boil again, and cook for 8–10 minutes until tender. Do not overcook. Drain in colander.
2. Meanwhile grate cheese.
3. In greased casserole arrange a layer of macaroni, then chili, then cheese. Repeat, ending with cheese.
4. Bake at 300° for 45 minutes.

May be made ahead and reheated at 350° for 20 minutes or until bubbly.

BAKED EGGS

4 ingredients

SERVES 4

1 cup mushroom soup
1½ cups bread crumbs (Canned type is fine.)
4 eggs
½ cup diced ham

Method:

1. Dilute mushroom soup with 1 cup of water.
2. Grease 4 individual baking dishes.
3. Sprinkle ¼ cup bread crumbs into each dish.
4. Break an egg into each and sprinkle with ⅛ cup ham.
5. Cover each with mushroom-soup mixture.
6. Sprinkle remaining bread crumbs over top.
7. Bake for 12–15 minutes, until eggs are set.

Serve at once!

SCALLOPED EGG CASSEROLE

4 ingredients

SERVES 2

4 hard-cooked eggs
1 8-oz. carton French onion dip (I use Kraft's French Onion Teez Dip.)
½ cup milk
½ cup cracker crumbs (Canned type is fine. I use Nabisco's Cracker Meal.)

Method:

1. Slice eggs into greased baking dish.
2. Dilute onion dip with milk, then spoon over eggs to cover.
3. Top with cracker crumbs.
4. Bake at 350° for 15–20 minutes, or until bubbly hot.

Note: This is a delicious casserole which becomes even more festive if prepared in individual baking dishes.

EGGS FLORENTINE

4 ingredients

SERVES 2 to 3

1 10-oz. pkg. frozen spinach
2 tbsp. melted butter
2 hard-cooked eggs, sliced
1 10½-oz. can condensed Cheddar cheese soup (I use Campbell.)

Method:
1. Cook spinach according to directions on package. Drain.
2. Melt butter in baking dish.
3. Arrange spinach in baking dish and cover with egg slices.
4. Top with cheese soup.
5. Bake for 20 minutes at 350° until bubbly.

PARTY EGGS FOR TWO

4 ingredients

SERVES 2

4 slices white bread
¼ lb. butter
4 eggs
1 tsp. seasoned salt (I use Lawry's.)

Method:
1. Cut centers out of bread with biscuit cutter. Discard centers.
2. Melt about 1 tablespoon butter in large skillet over medium heat. When bubbling, lay 2 slices bread in pan.
3. Break an egg into each hole, and pierce the yolk. Sprinkle with seasoned salt.

4. When egg begins to set, turn slices over and fry the other side until light brown. Add more butter as needed to fry the bread.
5. Repeat process for other two pieces of bread.

Note: Serve piping hot. Nice with hot chocolate.

SCRAMBLED EGGS WITH COTTAGE CHEESE

3 ingredients

SERVES 6

12 eggs
1 cup cottage cheese with chives (Available in the dairy section of your market.)
¼ lb. butter

Method:
1. Beat eggs. Season to taste.
2. Fold in cottage cheese until well blended.
3. Cook in melted butter in large skillet until eggs are just set. Don't overcook. (Eggs continue cooking after you remove from heat.) They should be served light and fluffy and piping hot.

Note: To cook "Scrambled Eggs Western Style," use 3 tablespoons Heinz's Chili Sauce instead of cottage cheese.

LIMA-BEAN CASSEROLE

4 ingredients

SERVES 3 to 4

1 10-oz. pkg. frozen baby lima beans
1 8-oz. pkg. small ready-cooked sausages
1 10½-oz. can white sauce (I use Aunt Penny's.)*
1 cup poultry dressing (I use Kellogg's Croutettes Stuffing.)

     *If unavailable in your area, *see recipe page 137.*

Method:
1. Cook lima beans according to directions on package, drain, and pour into buttered casserole.
2. Cut sausages in inch pieces, brown in skillet, then arrange over beans.
3. Add white sauce to pan drippings, stir until blended, and pour over beans.
4. Chop the poultry dressing fine and cover all ingredients.
5. Bake for 20 minutes at 350°.

HURRY-UP MACARONI AND CHEESE

3 ingredients

SERVES 4

1 cup macaroni
1 10½-oz. can condensed Cheddar cheese soup (I use Campbell.)
1 cup onion-flavored snack rings (I use "Onyums," a General Mills product.)

Method:
1. Cook macaroni in boiling, salted water for 8–10 minutes. Drain.
2. Combine macaroni and soup in buttered baking dish.
3. Crumble onion rings and sprinkle on top.
4. Bake in slow (300°) oven for 20–30 minutes until heated through and onion rings are golden brown.

PORK CHOP-BUTTER BEAN CASSEROLE

4 ingredients

SERVES 4

4 center-cut pork chops
1 10½-oz. can white sauce*
1 24-oz. can butter beans with ham (I use Libby.)
1 cup cracker crumbs (I use saltines.)

* If unavailable in your area, *see recipe page 137.*

Method:
1. Brown chops, then remove to baking dish.
2. Add white sauce to pan drippings. Cook for a few minutes, stirring to mix in brown bits in pan which add flavor.
3. Pour butter beans on top of chops, then pour gravy over them.
4. Sprinkle cracker crumbs on top.
5. Bake at 350° for 30–40 minutes until bubbling hot. Crumbs should be lightly browned.

SAUSAGE-POTATO BAKE

4 ingredients

SERVES 2

1 8-oz. pkg. sausages (8 to 10)
2 tbsp. flour
1 cup milk
2 medium potatoes

Method:
1. Cook sausages in skillet until brown. Remove and drain on paper towels. Reserve drippings.
2. Add flour to drippings and blend.
3. Add milk and cook until smooth, being sure to scrape the delicious crusty pieces into the gravy.
4. Arrange sausages in bottom of greased baking dish. Slice potatoes and arrange over sausages, then pour gravy over all.
5. Bake at 350° for 1 hour, or until potatoes are cooked.

If assembled and refrigerated in advance, increase baking time to 1¼ hours.

MEXICAN PARTY CASSEROLE

4 ingredients

SERVES 4 to 6

2 1-lb. cans beans and ground beef in barbecue sauce (I use Campbell.)
1 cup whole kernel corn, flavored with green and red sweet peppers (I use Mexicorn made by Green Giant.)
¼ cup sliced, ripe olives
1 cup shredded, mild cheese (I use Velveeta.)

Optional: ½ cup each chopped onion and sliced celery

Method:
1. Combine beans and ground beef, corn, olives, and if you like, onion and celery.
2. Pour into greased 1½-quart casserole.
3. Sprinkle cheese over top.
4. Bake at 300° for 45 minutes, or until bubbling hot.

May be made in advance, refrigerated, then reheated for 20–30 minutes in 300° oven until bubbly.

SCALLOP CASSEROLE

4 ingredients

SERVES 2

1 8-oz. pkg. frozen scallops
1 10½-oz. can condensed cream-of-mushroom soup
2 tbsp. bottled, imitation crumbled bacon (Usually found in spice section of market. I use French's.)
1 cup cracker crumbs (I use saltines or Nabisco's Cracker Meal.)

Method:
1. Defrost scallops.
2. Cover with mushroom soup, then bacon.
3. Top with cracker crumbs.
4. Bake at 400° for 15–20 minutes, or until crackers are light brown on top.

   Note: A whisper of herb seasoning is good, about ¼ tsp. (I use Lawry's Pinch of Herbs.)

SHEPHERD'S PIE

4 ingredients

SERVES 4

1 pkg. Birds Eye Mixed Vegetables with Onion Sauce (corn, carrots, green beans, peas, baby lima beans)
2 cups leftover lamb
2 10½-oz. cans mushroom gravy
2 cups mashed potatoes (packaged or leftover)

Method:
1. Cook vegetables according to directions on package.
2. Chop lamb into small pieces.
3. Combine lamb, vegetables, and gravy, and pour into buttered casserole.
4. Top with mashed potatoes. Roughen the top with a fork.
5. Bake at 400° for 30–40 minutes until peaks of potatoes are brown.

DEEP-DISH SHRIMP PIES

4 ingredients

SERVES 8

3 tbsp. flour
1 14½-oz. can stewed tomatoes (These are seasoned with celery, onions, spices, etc.)
3 lbs. fresh shrimp
1 15-oz. box corn muffin mix (I use Dromedary.)

Method:
1. Mix flour thoroughly with 3 tablespoons of juice from tomatoes, then add to tomatoes and cook until mixture thickens.
2. Clean and devein shrimp.
3. Add shrimp to sauce and cook for 1 minute or until pink and firm.
4. Pour into 8 individual casseroles.*
5. Make corn muffin mix according to directions on package. Spread 1 rounded tablespoon of batter over mixture in each casserole.
6. Bake for 30–40 minutes in 375° oven until topping is light brown.

* Individual casseroles come in all price ranges. Very practical, inexpensive, oven-proof ones are usually available in dime stores.

PANTRY-SHELF TUNA CASSEROLE

4 ingredients

SERVES 2 to 3

1 9¼-oz. can white-meat tuna
1 cup sandwich spread (I use Kraft.)
1 3-oz. can water chestnuts
½ cup crisp Chinese noodles

Method:
1. Cut up tuna into bite-size pieces, approximately ¾-inch square.
2. Combine sandwich spread with 1 cup of water.
3. Slice or chop water chestnuts and add to spread mixture.
4. Fold in tuna gently so as not to break up further.
5. Sprinkle Chinese noodles on top.
6. Bake in greased casserole at 325° for 20–30 minutes or until bubbly hot.

Main Courses

BEEF STROGANOFF

4 ingredients

SERVES 6

1½ lbs. filet of beef steak
½ lb. butter
½ lb. fresh mushrooms
1 pt. dairy sour cream

Optional: 1 cup finely sliced onions cooked in butter

Method:

1. With sharp knife cut filet into *very thin* slices, then cut each slice into strips as for French fries. They will measure about 2–3 inches long by ¼-inch wide.
2. Melt 1 stick butter in heavy skillet. At medium-high heat, sauté beef strips, a few at a time, removing to platter as soon as lightly browned. (If you try to sauté them all at one time, they simmer in their juices rather than browning properly.)
3. Slice mushrooms vertically through cap and stems.
4. Add a little more butter as needed to sauté mushrooms until soft and brown. Remove mushrooms.
5. Add sour cream to pan drippings, being sure to scrape all the good little brown bits into gravy.
6. Add the meat and mushrooms and heat.

Serve over rice or noodles.

DE LUXE BEEF-TENDERLOIN ROAST

4 ingredients

SERVES 4 to 6

2 tbsp. bottled browning sauce (I use Kitchen Bou-
quet.)

3-lb. piece tenderloin (Same as filet mignon except
all in one piece. Ask for a uniform piece,* so that
it will roast evenly.)

1 tsp. seasoned salt (I use Lawry's.)

1 tsp. lemon-pepper marinade (I use Lawry's.)

> * A whole beef tenderloin weighs about 4–6 lbs. and makes
> 8–12 1-inch thick filet mignon steaks. A half tenderloin
> (2–3 lbs.) is more often available. Though more often served
> as steak, it is almost without peer, served as a roast.
>
> There are superior cuts of tenderloin, as is the case with
> any other meat cut. Sometimes it's quite large at one end
> and small at the other. For roasting purposes, it's better to
> get it as uniform as possible. The meat man will usually
> oblige if you explain that it's to be roasted.

Method:

1. Rub browning sauce over the roast.
2. Sprinkle with seasoned salt and pepper.
3. Roast, uncovered, at 325° for about 45 minutes to 1 hour,
   depending on how well done you like it. For medium-rare,
   meat thermometer will register 150°. At this temperature,
   meat should be brown on outside and delicately pink on inside. (If in doubt, cut into center portion to see.)

I put meat in oven when guests arrive so that it is roasting
as we have drinks.

Note: Awfully good with Horseradish Mousse, *page 136.*

CAREFREE CHICKEN FOR 2

4 ingredients

SERVES 2

2 chicken breasts
1 10½-oz. can cream-of-celery soup
1⅓ cups Minute Rice
2 tbsp. dry onion soup (I use Lipton.)

Method:
1. Place chicken breasts in casserole.
2. Add ½ can of water to celery soup.
3. Mix rice, celery soup, and dry onion soup, then pour over chicken.
4. Bake covered for 20 minutes at 350°, then uncovered for 30 minutes or until brown on top.

CHICKEN ALMOND

4 ingredients

SERVES 4

4–5 lb. stewing chicken
5 or 6 green onions
4 tbsp. cornstarch
1 cup salted almonds

Optional: ½ green pepper, chopped

Method:
1. Cut up chicken and simmer in 4 cups of water in deep kettle or Dutch oven for 3–4 hours or until fork-tender. Add more water if needed.
2. As soon as it is cool enough for handling, strip the chicken meat from the bones, discarding skin. Cut into bite-sized pieces.
3. Cool the chicken broth. Skim chicken fat off top and place in small skillet. Reserve the broth.
4. Simmer chopped green onions (and chopped green peppers, if desired) in small amount of the chicken fat, until soft. Remove the onions and set them aside.
5. Blend 4 tablespoons of chicken fat or butter with 4 tablespoons of cornstarch by stirring over low heat. Add 2 cups chicken broth and stir until smooth.
6. Add chicken, onions, and almonds to gravy. Serve over rice. (If more liquid is needed, add canned chicken broth.)

CHICKEN CREOLE LOUISIANNE

3 ingredients

SERVES 6 to 8

2 2½–3 lb. ready-to-cook broiler-fryers
4–6 tbsp. butter
1 15½-oz. can sandwich sauce (I use Hunt's Manwich or 1 cup bottled barbecue sauce.)

Method:
1. Cut chickens into serving pieces. Pat dry with paper towels.
2. Melt butter and rub on each piece.
3. Brown chicken, skin sides down, in 400° oven for 20 minutes, in 9 x 13-inch baking dish.
4. Turn chicken, skin side up, spoon sandwich or barbecue sauce over chicken.
5. Continue baking for 20 minutes or until fork-tender.

CHICKEN KIEV

4 ingredients

SERVES 2

2 whole chicken breasts (boned by butcher if possible)
¼ lb. butter (Use an individually wrapped stick.)
2 cups dry bread crumbs (Packaged type is fine.)
1 cup homogenized shortening (I use Crisco.)

Optional: ½ cup chopped chives*

* Chopped chives are available in 2-oz. cartons in the frozen-food section of most markets. If you wish to use in this dish, sprinkle about 1 tsp. on each breast before rolling up.

Method:

1. Separate meat from bones if butcher has not done it for you. It comes away easily. Discard skin. Cut each breast in half.
2. Cover each chicken piece with wax paper and pound with flat mallet or rolling pin, until about ¼-inch thick.
3. Cut well-chilled butter in half lengthwise, then cut lengthwise again so that each of 4 pieces measures about 3 x ¼ x ¼ inches.
4. Lay a stick of butter on each of the 4 sections of chicken, tuck in the ends over butter, and roll tightly so that butter is entirely enclosed by chicken. Tie securely with white twine or heavy thread.
5. Roll in crumbs and chill in refrigerator until cooking time.
6. Heat shortening to 370° (preferably in electric skillet), drop in chicken pieces and shallow fry for approximately 5 minutes on each side or until golden brown.
7. Remove twine and serve piping hot.

CHICKEN-MUSHROOM BAKE

3 ingredients

SERVES 2

2 chicken breasts, cut in half to make 4 pieces
1 10½-oz. can condensed cream-of-mushroom soup
½ cup white wine

Method:
1. Arrange chicken, cut side down, in buttered baking dish.
2. Combine soup and wine and pour over chicken.
3. Bake uncovered for 45 minutes to 1 hour at 350° until fork-tender.

CORNISH HEN AND MUSHROOMS

4 ingredients

SERVES 2

1 Cornish game hen
4 tbsp. butter
6 fresh mushrooms
1 10½-oz. can condensed cream-of-chicken soup

Method:
1. Cut game hen in half and dry with paper towel.
2. Brown pieces in 3 tbsp. butter in large skillet. Place in baking dish.
3. Slice mushrooms vertically through caps and stems and brown in remaining 1 tbsp. butter. Spread on top of game hen.
4. Add chicken soup to pan drippings, being sure to stir brown bits into gravy. Pour over game hen and mushrooms.
5. Bake at 350° for 45 minutes or until tender.

CREOLE MEAT LOAF

4 ingredients

SERVES 4

    1 5-oz. can water chestnuts
    1 egg
    ½ cup chili sauce (I use Heinz.)
    1 lb. ground round steak

Method:
1. Thinly slice water chestnuts.
2. Slightly beat egg.
3. Combine all ingredients. Form into loaf.
4. Turn into greased loaf pan 9 x 5 x 3 inches. Leave at least ½-inch space between meat and sides of pan so that loaf will brown properly.
5. Bake at 400° for 1 hour.

GARLIC-HERB LEG O' LAMB

3 ingredients

SERVES 6 to 8

    1 1½-oz. pkg. garlic-herb salad dressing (I use Schilling's.)
    ½ cup salad oil (I use Mazola corn oil.)
    3-lb. leg of lamb

Method:
1. Mix salad dressing and salad oil.
2. Pour over lamb and allow to marinate for 20–30 minutes or longer, turning meat in marinade.
3. Roast at 350° for approximately 2 hours. Meat thermometer should register 175°.

GOOD GOOP

4 ingredients

SERVES 4 to 6

4 slices bacon
4 frankfurters
1 cup stewed tomatoes (These are seasoned with celery, onions, spices, etc.)
1½ cups grated Cheddar cheese

Optional: 1 cup pitted ripe olives cut in half

Method:
1. Cut bacon into 1-inch slices and fry until crisp. Remove bacon and drain off fat from pan.
2. Cut frankfurters into ½-inch pieces and place in pan along with tomatoes. Heat thoroughly.
3. Add cheese, bacon, and olives if desired. Cook over very low heat until cheese is melted. Spoon over toast or rolls.

Note: Good Goop is especially popular with teen-agers.

MEAT-LOAF RING

4 ingredients

SERVES 4

2 eggs
2 lbs. ground round steak
1 1½-oz. pkg. dry meat-loaf seasoning mix (I use Schilling's or Lawry's.)
½ cup chili sauce (I use Heinz.)

Method:
1. Beat eggs.
2. Mix together ground round, beaten eggs, and meat-loaf seasoning mix.
3. Spoon mixture into buttered ring mold.
4. Spread chili sauce over top. Bake in preheated oven at 375° for 45 minutes or until meat browns and shrinks from sides of pan.

   Note: A loaf pan may be used if preferred. Bake for an extra 15 or 20 minutes.

BREADED PORK STEAKS

4 ingredients

SERVES 2 to 3

1½ lbs. center-cut pork (no bone)
1 egg
1 cup fine dry bread crumbs
1 cup homogenized shortening (I use Crisco.)

Method:
1. Cut meat into serving pieces, and pound with flat mallet or with a tenderizer utensil. (They will increase in size to almost double.)
2. Beat egg with 2 tablespoons of water.
3. Dip meat in egg mixture, roll in crumbs, and chill for 30 minutes before frying.
4. Heat shortening in heavy skillet to 370° or until a cube of bread will brown in 60 seconds.
5. Cook meat until golden brown on both sides. Drain on paper towels. Salt and pepper to taste.

   Note: If you wish, remove to warmed platter and garnish with slices of lemon, crisp lettuce, and sliced sweet pickles.

GONE-FOR-THE-DAY POT ROAST

4 ingredients

SERVES 10 to 12

3–4 lbs. sirloin-tip pot roast
3 tbsp. shortening
½ cup seasoned cooking sherry (I use Reese's Sherry Cooking Wine.)
1 ⅘-oz. pkg. garlic-herb dressing mix

Method:
1. In Dutch oven, on top of stove, brown roast in shortening on all sides.
2. Combine sherry with dressing mix and pour over roast.
3. Roast at 175° in oven, covered, for 8 to 10 hours.

Note: It won't hurt it to cook longer if you are delayed. Wonderful flavor. Good with buttered noodles.

BEEF SHANK POT ROAST

3 ingredients

SERVES 6

5–6 lbs. beef shank, all in one piece if possible*
1 can mushroom soup (I use Campbell's Golden Mushroom.)
1 pkg. Lipton's Onion Soup Mix

* Other cuts of beef may be substituted such as eye round, rump, boned and rolled chuck roast, beef short ribs, etc.

Method:

1. Measure a piece of heavy-duty aluminum foil about twice the size of the meat.
2. Set meat in center of foil.
3. Pour over meat the mushroom soup, then the onion soup mix.
4. Bring foil up around the meat, sealing it by folding ends under at top and sides, then folding ends under a second time.
5. Place foil-wrapped meat on shallow baking dish and roast at 300° for 4–5 hours.

Note: The combined soups and meat juices make a delicious gravy for noodles or mashed potatoes.

Leftover roast may be served cold, made into beef stew or soup, or sliced for sandwiches.

SALMON FLUFF

4 ingredients

SERVES 3

6 eggs
1 cup sandwich spread (I use Heinz.)
1 cup red salmon (Crabmeat, shrimp, or lobster may be substituted.)
½ tsp. cream of tartar

Method:

1. Beat 4 egg yolks until lemon-colored. (Save 2 remaining yolks for other uses.)
2. Combine with sandwich spread.
3. Remove skin and bones from salmon, then gently combine the salmon with the sauce.

4. Beat 6 egg whites with cream of tartar until stiff, then fold into the other mixture.
5. Pour into 1½-qt. ungreased baking dish or soufflé dish.
6. Bake at 375° for 30–35 minutes until delicately brown.

Serve at once!

SALMON WIGGLE

4 ingredients

SERVES 3 to 4

1-lb. can red salmon
2 pkgs. frozen peas and pearl onions in cream sauce (I use Birds Eye.)
8 toast cups
1 cup milk (approx.)

Method:
1. Flake salmon, removing pieces of dark skin and bones.
2. Prepare vegetables as directed on package.
3. Make toast cups by cutting crusts from slices of fresh white bread, then fitting them into muffin cups. Bake in 400° oven until brown on edges (about 8 minutes).
4. Combine salmon and vegetables. Add enough milk so that mixture is of pouring consistency, about like medium white sauce. Cook over low heat until bubbling hot.
5. Spoon mixture into hot toast cups and serve at once.

SHRIMP CREOLE

4 ingredients

SERVES 6

2½ lbs. fresh shrimp
1 lb. fresh mushrooms
⅛ lb. butter
1 14½-oz. can stewed tomatoes (These are seasoned
with celery, onions, spices, etc.)

Method:
1. Clean and devein shrimp.
2. Sauté mushrooms in butter.
3. Add stewed tomatoes to mushrooms and cook together for 2 or
3 minutes. Salt and pepper to taste. Set aside.
4. Just before serving, bring sauce to a boil, add shrimp, and
cook for about 1 minute—until shrimp are pink and firm.
5. Serve over hot cooked rice.

SUKIYAKI

4 ingredients

SERVES 6

1½ lbs. filet mignon steak
2 tbsp. fat or a small piece of suet
2 pkgs. Birds Eye Japanese Style Vegetables (This
item is from their collection of international recipes. The package contains thinly sliced green
beans, onions, broccoli, and mushrooms in a seasoned sauce.)
Cooked rice

Optional: soy sauce to pass

Method:
1. Cut steak into very thin slices, about ¼-inch, with a sharp knife.
2. Heat skillet until quite hot. Melt suet or fat.
3. Brown the meat on both sides. This will only take a few seconds as it is cut so thin.
4. Cook Japanese Style Vegetables according to directions on package. Do not overcook. They should be on the crisp side.
5. Combine the meat and vegetables and bring to boil.
6. Serve bubbling hot over rice. Guests add soy sauce if they wish.

THREE-LAYER SPARERIBS BAKE

3 ingredients

SERVES 2 to 3

2 lbs. spareribs
2 cups sauerkraut
2 cups applesauce

Method:
1. Brown ribs in a 9 x 13-inch baking dish for 15 minutes in 400° oven, then turn heat down to 350°.
2. Spoon sauerkraut over ribs.
3. Spoon applesauce over sauerkraut.
4. Bake for 1 hour.

Note: If you prefer, use center-cut pork chops in place of ribs.

VEAL BIRDS

4 ingredients

SERVES 6

> 6 pieces thinly sliced veal about ¼″ thick (approx.
> 1½ lbs.)
> 1½ cups poultry stuffing (I use Kellogg's Croutettes
> Stuffing.)
> 2 tbsp. vegetable oil (I use Wesson.)
> ¾ cup bottled creamy onion dressing (I use Wish-
> bone's California Onion.)

Method:

1. With a rolling pin, roll veal pieces as thin as possible.
2. Place ¼ cup stuffing on each, roll each slice up like a jelly roll, and fasten with toothpicks or tie with string.
3. Heat oil in skillet and sauté veal until lightly browned on all sides. Remove to platter.
4. Add salad dressing to drippings and stir to blend with all brown, crusty bits in pan.
5. Place birds in baking dish, cover with sauce, and bake at 350° for 1 hour.
6. Remove string or toothpicks before serving.

If assembled in advance and refrigerated, increase roasting time to 1¼ hours.

Relishes

BLEU CHEESE MOUSSE

3 ingredients

SERVES 4

1 pt. heavy cream
½ lb. bleu cheese
1 tbsp. grated onion

Optional: ½ tsp. freshly ground pepper

Method:
1. Whip cream.
2. Mix cheese with a little cream to make a soft paste. Add cheese and onion to cream and whip again. It need not be completely free of lumps. You may use blender. Add a little freshly ground pepper if you wish.
3. Half fill paper cups and freeze. Just before serving, remove paper cups and serve on lettuce leaf.

Note: May be used as a salad, or as an accompaniment to meat.

HORSERADISH MOUSSE

4 ingredients

SERVES 6

1½ tbsp. unflavored gelatin
1 cup sour cream
1 cup prepared horseradish (or less if you like it milder)
1 tbsp. chopped onion

Method:
1. In top part of double boiler mix gelatin in ¼ cup of cold water. Place pan over boiling water until gelatin is dissolved.
2. Cool slightly. Add remaining ingredients. Season to taste.
3. Pour into mold and chill for several hours until firm.

Note: Very good with roast beef or cold cuts.

ORANGE-CRANBERRY RELISH

3 ingredients

YIELD: 3 to 4 cups

2 oranges
1 16-oz. pkg. (4 cups) cranberries
2 cups sugar

Method:
1. Use medium blade of food chopper and grind together oranges and cranberries.
2. Add sugar.
3. Store in refrigerator. May be frozen if desired.

Note: Wonderful with roast turkey or chicken. Delicious as a spread on toast.

WHITE SAUCE

3 ingredients

YIELD: 1 cup

Medium white sauce:
2 tbsp. margarine or butter
2 tbsp. flour
1 cup milk

Thin white sauce:
1 tbsp. margarine or butter ·
1 tbsp. flour
1 cup milk

Thick white sauce:
4 tbsp. margarine or butter
4 tbsp. flour
1 cup milk

Method:
1. Melt butter in skillet over medium heat.
2. Add flour and stir until smooth.
3. Add milk and continue stirring constantly over medium heat until smooth and thickened. Season to taste with salt and/or pepper if desired.

Rice and Macaroni Dishes

NOODLES ALFREDO

3 ingredients

SERVES 4

8-oz. pkg. fettucini noodles (very fine)
¼ lb. butter
1 cup Parmesan cheese, grated

Method:
1. Cook noodles according to directions on package.
2. Drain well, then toss with butter and cheese.
3. Serve immediately.

Note: This is especially good when served with Italian specialties such as Chicken Cacciatore or Veal Scaloppine.

Noodles Alfredo also makes a nice change when substituted for potatoes with many of the main dishes in this book such as Pot Roast, Swiss Steak, Veal Birds, Meat Loaf, Carefree Chicken, Fish Fry Almondine. *See Index for page numbers.*

BAKED NOODLES ROMANOFF

4 ingredients

SERVES 4

 1 5-oz. pkg. noodles (I use medium egg noodles.)
 1 cup sour cream
 1 cup cottage cheese
 ½ cup grated Parmesan cheese

   Optional: seasoned salt, Worcestershire sauce, etc.

Method:
1. Cook noodles in boiling salted water until tender (about 10 minutes). Drain, then rinse with cold water.
2. Add sour cream, cottage cheese, and seasonings if desired.
3. Pour into greased baking dish or ring mold, and sprinkle with Parmesan cheese.
4. Bake at 350° for 45 minutes or until brown and crusty.

If assembled in advance and refrigerated, increase baking time to 1 hour.

Note: Serve as an accompaniment to meat—or if using ring mold, fill center with creamed fish, eggs, or chicken.

RICE CHEESE RING

3 ingredients

SERVES 4

 4½ cups cooked rice
 ¼ cup melted butter or margarine
 1 cup grated sharp Cheddar cheese

Method:
1. Combine all ingredients. Pack into a well-greased ring mold.
2. Bake in a hot (400°) oven for 15–20 minutes.
3. Unmold on hot platter and fill with any creamed dish such as creamed tuna, chicken à la king, creamed mixed vegetables, etc.

If assembled and refrigerated ahead of time, increase baking time to 30 minutes.

MOCK WILD RICE

3 ingredients

SERVES 4

1 cup cracked wheat
4–6 tbsp. butter or margarine
1 1¾-oz. envelope chicken-noodle soup mix (I use Lipton.)

Method:
1. Wash cracked wheat in fine sieve. Drain well.
2. Melt butter over low heat in large skillet or chicken fryer, stirring constantly for about 7 or 8 minutes.
3. Add 3 cups boiling water and chicken-noodle soup mix and simmer for about 7 minutes, then add cracked wheat.
4. Transfer to baking dish and bake uncovered for 1 hour at 325°.

The finished product should be on the dry side.

Note: Wonderful with chicken recipes or with lamb shish kabob.

HURRY-UP SPAGHETTI

4 ingredients

SERVES 3 to 4

1 lb. ground round steak
½ cup green pepper
1 15¼-oz. can spaghetti in tomato sauce (I use Franco American.)
1 cup grated sharp Cheddar cheese

Optional: You may add any number of things to this dish: onions, mushrooms, ripe olives, corn niblets, etc.

Method:
1. Cook ground steak in heavy skillet, over medium-high heat, a little at a time to insure browning properly. Lift out with slotted spoon and drain.
2. Cut pepper into small pieces.
3. Brown pepper in meat drippings until slightly soft. Discard meat grease, if any.
4. Add canned spaghetti, meat, and cheese and toss all lightly together. Heat until bubbly.

SPAGHETTI TROYER

4 ingredients

SERVES 4

2 cups leftover ham
1 large green pepper
1 16-oz. pkg. spaghetti #8 size
4 medium eggs

Optional: grated Parmesan cheese

Method:
1. Cut ham into 1-inch cubes and cut pepper into small pieces.
2. Simmer ham and green pepper in ½ cup water in heavy skillet for 5 minutes.
3. Cook spaghetti in boiling salted water to the "al dente" (barely tender) stage (about 7 minutes). Drop 3 or 4 ice cubes into water to prevent further cooking. Drain.
4. Pour spaghetti over ham and pepper in skillet and stir gently.
5. Turn burner to medium heat.
6. Beat eggs.
7. Pour beaten eggs over mixture and cook until eggs are set (about 2 or 3 minutes).

Note: Extra good if you sprinkle each serving with about 1 tsp. grated Parmesan cheese.

Salads

BACON-ROMAINE SALAD

4 ingredients

SERVES 6 to 8

2 heads romaine
1 lb. bacon
1 cup bottled bleu cheese dressing (I use Lawry's.)
1 cup croutons (I use Kellogg's Croutettes Stuffing.)

> *Optional:* peeled tomatoes and/or sliced, hard-cooked eggs

Method:
1. Fill sink with cold water, cut off stem of romaine and wash leaves well. Roll in paper towels to dry thoroughly and chill well in refrigerator.
2. With kitchen shears, cut bacon crosswise into 1-inch slices. Fry in large skillet until crisp. Drain on paper towels.
3. Just before serving, pour desired amount of dressing over greens. (Leaves should be coated, but not ''drowned'' in dressing.)
4. Sprinkle bacon over leaves. Add tomatoes and/or eggs, if desired.
5. At last minute sprinkle croutons over all, then toss lightly.

COLE SLAW

3 ingredients

SERVES 4 to 6

1 large cabbage
1 onion, preferably sweet Bermuda (You may use 1 small can of crushed pineapple instead of onion.)
1 cup bottled cole-slaw dressing (I use Kraft.)

Method:
1. Chop or grate cabbage (I prefer the old-fashioned chopping method in the wooden bowl. It leaves the cabbage much finer in texture.)
2. Mince onion very fine and add to cabbage.
3. Add dressing just to moisten.
4. Refrigerate for several hours until thoroughly chilled.

May be made the day before serving if desired.

SPEEDY CRANBERRY GELATIN MOLD

3 ingredients

SERVES 4

1 3-oz. pkg. lemon gelatin
1 cup orange-cranberry relish (Make your own, *see page 136*, or buy at market.)
½ cup cottage cheese

Method:
1. Dissolve lemon gelatin in ¾ cup boiling water.
2. Cool slightly.
3. Add cranberry relish and cottage cheese.
4. Pour into greased mold. Refrigerate for several hours.
5. Unmold on bed of shredded lettuce. Garnish with mayonnaise if desired.

CRANBERRY-RASPBERRY MOLD

3 ingredients

SERVES 4 to 6

1 3-oz. pkg. raspberry gelatin
1 16-oz. can cranberry sauce (whole berries—Ocean Spray's Cranberry-Raspberry Jelly may be used in place of the whole-berry type)
1½ cups sour cream

Method:
1. Dissolve gelatin in 1 cup hot water.
2. Mix all ingredients together, using hands if necessary to make them blend. The mixture will not be completely smooth.
3. Pour into greased mold and chill in refrigerator for several hours or overnight. Serve on lettuce leaf if desired.

CREAM-OF-CUCUMBER SALAD

4 ingredients

SERVES 4 to 6

2 cucumbers
¼-oz. pkg. unflavored gelatin (I use Knox.)
¾ cup Italian dressing (I use Milani's 1890 or Kraft.)
½ pt. French onion dip (I use Kraft's French Onion Teez Dip.)

Method:
1. Cut cucumbers into 1-inch cubes.
2. Dissolve gelatin in 1 tbsp. cold water.
3. Heat Italian dressing, add gelatin, and mix well.

4. Cool until slightly jelled, add cucumbers and French onion dip and mix gently.
5. Place in refrigerator for several hours until well set.

Note: You can make your own onion dip by combining 1 cup dairy sour cream with ½ package of Lipton's dry onion soup mix or with 1 tbsp. *very* finely minced onion.

MOLDED EGG SALAD

4 ingredients

SERVES 8

6 hard-cooked eggs
2 ¼-oz. pkgs. unflavored gelatin (I use Knox.)
1 cup bottled cole-slaw dressing (I use Kraft.)
½ cup bottled hamburger relish or green India relish (I use Heinz.)

Method:
1. Slice eggs and arrange in mold or bowl.
2. Add ½ cup cold water to gelatin to soften, then 1½ cups boiling water and stir until dissolved.
3. Add gelatin mix to dressing and hamburger relish. Stir well. Pour over eggs.
4. Place in refrigerator until well set (for several hours or overnight). Serve on romaine.

ELKHORN KIDNEY-BEAN SALAD

4 ingredients

SERVES 4

1 15-oz. can dark red kidney beans (I use Stokeley Van Camp.)
1 medium-large onion
1 4-oz. jar sweet pickles
1 cup bottled Thousand Island dressing (I use Lawry's), or substitute oil and vinegar dressing (I use Kraft.)

Method:
1. Drain kidney beans.
2. Finely chop onion.
3. Dice pickles.
4. Combine beans, onion, and pickles.
5. Heat dressing, but do not boil.
6. Pour hot dressing over salad ingredients and toss until well coated.
7. Refrigerate until serving time.

May be made ahead.

GARDEN-PATCH SALAD

4 ingredients

SERVES 4

1 3-oz. pkg. lemon gelatin
½ cup lemon juice and grated rind
1 pkg. frozen mixed vegetables
½ cup (approx.) Thousand Island dressing (I use Kraft.)

Optional: lettuce or romaine

Method:
1. Mix gelatin with 1 cup boiling water.
2. Add lemon juice and rind to gelatin mix. Let cool until slightly thickened.
3. Cook vegetables according to directions on package. Drain.
4. Add vegetables to gelatin mixture.
5. Pour into mold and chill in refrigerator for several hours.
6. Unmold on chilled plate and, if you like, garnish with lettuce around the edge of plate. To serve, cut in pie-shaped wedges. Top with dressing.

GRAPEFRUIT ASPIC

4 ingredients

SERVES 4

1 1-lb. can grapefruit sections
¾ cup orange juice (approx.)
1¼-oz. envelope unflavored gelatin
½ cup bottled vinaigrette dressing (I use Bernstein. If you prefer a dressing not quite so tart, use Lawry's or Kraft's Thousand Island.)

Optional: ripe avocado, sliced

Method:
1. Drain grapefruit thoroughly, saving juice. Measure the amount of juice, then add enough orange juice to make a total of 1½ cups.
2. Mix gelatin with a little juice, then add balance of juice and heat until just under the boil.
3. Arrange grapefruit in a salad mold.
4. When juice has cooled a little, pour it over grapefruit and chill in refrigerator for several hours or until well set.
5. Unmold and serve plain with vinaigrette dressing or garnish with slices of ripe avocado.

GREEN ASPIC SALAD

4 ingredients

SERVES 10 to 12

1 6-oz. pkg. lime gelatin
1 cup blanched almonds
1 cucumber
2 ½-pt. cartons French onion dip (I use Kraft's French Onion Teez Dip.)

Optional: seedless green grapes

Method:
1. Dissolve gelatin in 1 cup hot water. Set aside.
2. Put almonds and cucumber through food chopper, using medium blade.
3. Combine all ingredients.
4. Pour into greased mold and chill in refrigerator for several hours or overnight.
5. Serve on lettuce and, if you wish, garnish with seedless green grapes.

Note: Serve small portions as this salad is very rich.

HOMEMADE MAYONNAISE

4 ingredients

YIELD: 1 cup

1 egg
2 tbsp. vinegar
1 tsp. seasoned salt (I use Lawry's.)
¾–1 cup salad oil (I use Mazola corn oil.)

Method:
1. Beat egg well at high speed in blender.
2. Add vinegar mixed with seasoned salt and blend.
3. Add a little oil and let blender run a minute or two at high speed. Gradually add remainder of oil, beating well after each addition. The mixture should be thick and smooth.

Note: If you prefer a somewhat sweeter dressing, add ½ tsp. sugar to the vinegar mixture.

FROZEN PEACH SALAD

3 ingredients

SERVES 6

1 21-oz. can peach pie filling (I use Wilderness.)
½ cup mayonnaise
1 cup sour cream

Method:
1. Combine ingredients.
2. Freeze in pie-filling can.
3. At serving time, remove mixture from can and slice in ¾″ slices. (Contents come out easily when bottom lid is removed.)
4. Serve individual portions on lettuce leaf.

Note: For weight watchers, beat 1 cup of cottage cheese until smooth and use in place of sour cream.

RED-AND-GREEN-PEPPER SALAD

4 ingredients

SERVES 4

2 sweet red peppers
2 sweet green peppers
1 large sweet Bermuda onion
½ cup bottled vinaigrette dressing (I use Bernstein's or Kraft's Oil & Vinegar.)

Method:
1. Remove seeds and ribs from peppers. Cut into thin slices.
2. Chop onion and add to peppers.
3. Pour dressing over onions and peppers and mix well. Cover and chill for several hours or overnight. Drain before serving.

ROQUEFORT SALAD DRESSING

4 ingredients

YIELD: 1¾ cups

1 3-oz. pkg. Roquefort cheese
½ cup sour cream or French onion dip (I use Kraft's French Onion Teez Dip.)
½ cup buttermilk
½ cup mayonnaise

Optional: ½ tsp. onion salt and/or ⅛ tsp. garlic powder

Method:
1. Use fork to blend Roquefort cheese and onion dip together.
2. Add buttermilk and mayonnaise and beat until smooth. Use blender if you prefer a very smooth dressing.
3. Make several hours ahead of time to allow flavors to blend. Store in covered jar in refrigerator.

SHRIMP OR CRAB LOUIS SALAD

4 ingredients

SERVES 2 to 3

1 4½-oz. can shrimp (6½-oz. can crabmeat may be substituted)
1 cup chopped celery
½ cup (approx.) bottled cole slaw or Thousand Island dressing (I use Kraft.)
2 hard-cooked eggs

Method:
1. Drain shrimp or crabmeat thoroughly.
2. Combine with celery and salad dressing.
3. Spoon into individual salad bowls and garnish with hard-cooked eggs. Serve on lettuce if desired.

STRAWBERRY GELATIN SALAD

4 ingredients

SERVES 12

2 bananas
1 6-oz. pkg. strawberry gelatin
2 10-oz. pkgs. frozen sliced strawberries
1 pt. pineapple yogurt

Method:
1. Mash bananas.
2. Dissolve gelatin in 3 cups boiling water.

3. Add strawberries and bananas and mix well. Pour into 9 x 13-inch baking pan.
4. Chill in refrigerator for several hours or until well set.
5. Frost top with yogurt and return to refrigerator until serving time.
6. To serve, cut into squares.

Note: May be used as salad or dessert.

Soups

NEW ENGLAND CLAM CHOWDER

4 ingredients

SERVES 6 to 8

6 slices bacon
1 16-oz. can potatoes
2 7½-oz. cans minced clams
1½ qts. milk

Optional: 1 tbsp. minced instant onion

Method:

1. Cut bacon crossways in approximately 1-inch slices.
2. Fry until crisp. Remove bacon with slotted spoon and set aside.
3. Cut potatoes into ½-inch cubes and fry in bacon drippings, then discard drippings.
4. Add clams and milk and onion, if desired, and heat. Season to taste. Ladle into bowls and sprinkle crisp bacon on top.

FRENCH ONION SOUP

4 ingredients

SERVES 4

4 medium onions (approx. 4 cups)
4 tbsp. butter
2 10½-oz. cans beef bouillon or consommé
2 tbsp. grated Parmesan cheese

Method:
1. Slice onions and fry in butter until *well* browned.
2. Dilute bouillon with 1½ cans water and add to onions. Simmer for 15 minutes.
3. Ladle into bowls. Sprinkle with cheese. Serve piping hot.

Note: For a heartier soup course ½ slice of French bread may be placed in each bowl and soup poured over it.

OYSTER STEW

4 ingredients

SERVES 2 to 3

1 8-oz. can small oysters
3 cups milk
2 tbsp. butter
Oyster crackers

Method:
1. Heat oysters, milk, and butter. Salt and pepper to taste.
2. Pour into bowls and top with 6 or 7 crackers.

SPLIT PEA SOUP

4 ingredients

SERVES 4

2 stalks celery
2 carrots
2 cups dry split peas (They come in a 16-oz. package.)
2 tbsp. onion soup mix (I use Lipton.)

  Optional: If you like, cook with a ham bone.

Method:
1. Chop celery and carrots.
2. Mix all ingredients. Add 2 quarts water in large kettle and simmer for 2–3 hours until peas are *very* soft.
3. Serve piping hot in heated bowls.

HOMEMADE VEGETABLE SOUP

4 ingredients

SERVES 4

3 beef shanks (approx. 2 lbs.)
4 stalks of celery
4 carrots
4 boiling potatoes

  Optional: 3 medium onions and/or 3–4 bouillon cubes

Method:

1. Cut off from beef as much fat as possible and simmer meat in 2 quarts water for 5–6 hours until very tender. Skim fat off top from time to time.
2. About 1 hour before serving, remove meat from broth and set aside. Peel vegetables, then slice. Add to hot broth and cook until tender. Onions and/or bouillon cubes may be used for added flavor.
3. When meat becomes cool enough to handle, remove it from bones and cut into bite-sized pieces. Return to broth and continue simmering with the vegetables. Season to taste.

Vegetables

ARTICHOKE BOTTOMS WITH BABY PEAS

4 ingredients

SERVES 4

    1 10-oz. pkg. frozen baby peas
    2 tbsp. butter
    ¼ lb. fresh mushrooms, chopped (3-oz. can chopped
      water chestnuts can be substituted)
    8 canned artichoke bottoms (Usually found in gour-
      met section of market.)

Method:
1. Cook peas according to directions on package.
2. Melt butter and cook mushrooms until soft. Add peas. Season to taste.
3. Heat artichoke bottoms. Drain and place on heated serving dish.
4. Fill artichoke bottoms with pea-mushroom combination.

Note: This is an excellent dish for buffet serving. The vegetables are delicious, look pretty on the platter, and are easy to handle.

STUFFED MUSHROOMS

3 ingredients

SERVES 4

8 medium fresh mushrooms
½ cup poultry stuffing (I use Kellogg's Croutettes Stuffing.)
4 tbsp. butter

Method:
1. Scrub mushrooms with soft brush and carefully remove stems. (They may be used later in another recipe.)
2. Place on baking sheet. Spoon 1 tablespoon chopped poultry stuffing into each mushroom cavity.
3. Melt butter and pour over mushrooms.
4. Bake at 350° for about 20 minutes or until stuffing browns.

FRENCH-FRIED ONIONS

4 ingredients

SERVES 4

4 large onions
1 cup milk
½ cup flour
2 cups salad oil (I use Mazola corn oil.)

Method:
1. Peel onions and cut into slices about ¼-inch thick.
2. Separate into rings and cover with milk. Let stand for 30 minutes.
3. Dip rings into flour, or shake in bag.
4. Heat salad oil to 380°.
5. Fry onion rings in oil a few at a time. When golden brown, remove to plate covered with paper towels. Sprinkle with salt. Keep hot in oven.

PATTYPAN SQUASH FILLED
WITH MEXICORN

4 ingredients

SERVES 4

8 pattypan squash (the scalloped, disk-shaped type)
1 12-oz. can Mexicorn, Green Giant brand
4 tsp. butter
Seasoned salt (I use Lawry's.)

Method:
1. Scrub squash well. Remove stem, but do not pare. Simmer for 15–20 minutes in water to cover. Scoop pulp from center, leaving a cup shape.
2. Drain Mexicorn. Combine with pulp.
3. Fill hollows in squash with mixture, heaping it up a little.
4. Top with ½ teaspoon butter and a sprinkle of seasoned salt.
5. Bake for 15–20 minutes at 350° until hot. Arrange on platter.

SPEEDY SPINACH SOUFFLÉ

4 ingredients

SERVES 4

1 pkg. frozen chopped spinach
1 10½-oz. can white sauce (1¼ cups)*
4 tbsp. bacon-onion bits (I use Lawry's Baconion.)
2 eggs

* If unavailable in your area, *see recipe page 137.*

Method:

1. Cook spinach according to directions on package. Pour into colander and drain *very well*. Force water out with back of spoon.
2. Lightly fold in white sauce and bacon-onion bits.
3. Beat eggs slightly with a folk and fold into spinach mixture. Do this lightly, just until ingredients are mixed together to provide a contrast between the dark green of the spinach and the pale yellow of the cream sauce.
4. Cook slowly on top of stove in heavy saucepan or skillet until eggs are set (about 5 minutes). Do not overcook.

SWEET-POTATO BALLS

4 ingredients

SERVES 3 to 4

2 medium sweet potatoes or yams
½ cup miniature marshmallows
1 cup liquid honey
1 cup chopped walnuts or pecans

Method:

1. Boil sweet potatoes in jackets until soft, then remove jackets and mash the potatoes. Chill.
2. Allow about ¼ cup for each ball. Insert a miniature marshmallow in center of each, and with buttered hands roll each into a ball.
3. Dip each ball into warmed honey, then shake in bag containing chopped nuts. Chill 30 minutes or longer.
4. Place on buttered baking sheet and bake in 350° oven for 20–30 minutes or until bubbling hot.

BAKED TOMATOES PARMESAN

4 ingredients

SERVES 4

4 medium or large tomatoes
¼ cup salad oil (I use Wesson or Mazola corn oil.)
4 tbsp. grated Parmesan cheese
4 tsp. bottled bacon-onion bits (I use Lawry's Bac-onion.)

Method:
1. Cut away stem end of tomatoes. Cut in half horizontally.
2. Brush cut halves with vegetable oil.
3. Spoon 1 tablespoon Parmesan cheese on each cut half.
4. Top each with 1 teaspoon bacon-onion bits.
5. Place on baking sheet and bake for 20 minutes at 350°.

Note: Nice with steak or fish.

SPRING MEDLEY OF VEGETABLES

4 ingredients

SERVES 4

6–8 new carrots
6–8 small, white onions, frozen or fresh
1 10-oz. pkg. Birds Eye frozen Green Peas and Potatoes with Cream Sauce
1 10½-oz. can white sauce (I use Aunt Penny's.)*

* If unavailable in your area, *see recipe page 137.*

Method:
1. Boil carrots and onions together in a large saucepan until tender, about 25–35 minutes. Drain.
2. Prepare peas and potatoes according to directions on package and combine with white sauce.
3. Gently combine all ingredients and heat until bubbly over medium heat. Watch carefully to avoid scorching. May be made in advance and refrigerated. Reheat in 325° oven 30 minutes.

Note: To make this a main course, add 2 cups of bite-sized pieces of cooked chicken, turkey, ham, or shrimp.

CHEESY ZUCCHINI AND TOMATOES

4 ingredients

SERVES 4

1 15-oz. can stewed tomatoes (These are seasoned with celery, onions, spices, etc.)
6–8 medium zucchinis
½ cup chopped onions
½ cup grated sharp Cheddar cheese

Method:
1. Drain stewed tomatoes well and discard juice.
2. Wash zucchinis, then cut into ½-inch slices and place in greased baking dish.
3. Stir in onions and tomatoes. Cover.
4. Bake at 350° for 30–40 minutes or until onions are soft.
5. Remove cover, sprinkle cheese on top, and broil a minute or two until cheese melts. Watch carefully to avoid scorching.

Index

almond recipes
    cherries jubilee almondine, 83
    chicken almond, 122–123
    chicken sandwich almondine, 74
    fish fry almondine, 38–39
    honey-almond sundae, 104
    nut macaroon wafers, 96–97
    pilaff, 42–43
    quick biscuit tortoni, 81
    Southern tipsy cake, 105
ambrosia, Hawaiian, 6
angel food cake
    with raspberries and whipped cream, 76
    in Southern tipsy cake, 105
appetizers, 55–62
    pineapple nibblers, 50
apple recipes
    applesauce-chocolate chip tart, 84
    applesauce quickie, 47
    fried apple rings, 52
    Persian delight, 44
    pie, 100–101
    red-cabbage-and-apple casserole, 30–31
    snow pudding, 77
    turnovers, 77–78
    Waldorf salad, 20
    See also cider
apricot crisp, 78
artichokes
    with baby peas, 158
    in salade niçoise, 12

aspic
    grapefruit, 148
    green, 149
    tomato, 46–47
avocados, *see* grapefruit aspic ; guacamole salad or dip

bacon recipes
    bacon bars, 69
    bacon-romaine salad, 143
    bacon-wrapped burgers, 46
    cheese dreams, 70
    eggs Benedict, 50–51
    glorified frankfurters, 30
    good goop, 127
    hot German potato salad, 31
    mystery gourmet sandwich, 75
    New England clam chowder, 154
    Rumakis, 59–60
    spinach-bacon salad, 16
baked Alaska dessert, 79
banana-coconut cream pie, 80
bananas
    baked, 79–80
    in strawberry gelatin salad, 152–153
barbecue dishes
    chicken creole Louisianne, 123
    shish kabobs, 42
    teriyaki strips, 55–56
bean salad, 147

caramel-nut ice cream balls, 14

carrots
in soups, 155–156
in vegetable medley, 162–163

casserole recipes, 107–111, 113–119
baked noodles Romanoff, 139
cheese, 16–17
escalloped ham and potatoes, 20
green bean, 9
red cabbage and apple, 30–31
scalloped onions, 35

cauliflower
escalloped, 6
in spinach-bacon salad, 16

celery
in Mexican party casserole, 116
in shrimp or crab salad, 152
in soups, 156–157
in Waldorf salad, 20

cheese ball appetizer, 56
cheese biscuits, tiny, 21
cheese casserole, 16–17
cheese dreams, 70
cheese mousse, bleu, 135
cheese pie, lemon-flavored, 94
cheese snacks, 56–57
cheese squares, 57
cheesecake, chocolate cream, 85–86

cheesy chicken, 12–13
cheesy zucchini and tomatoes, 163
cherries jubilee almondine, 83
cherry graham-cracker pudding, 18

chicken
almond, 122–123
breasts in casserole, 107–108
cheesy, 12–13
creole Louisianne, 123
divan, 108
Kiev, 124
minced, in sandwiches, 74
mushroom bake, 125

chicken livers, see Rumakis
chili-macaroni casserole, 109
chocolate-chip tart shells, 84
chocolate-chip tortes, 83–84
chocolate cookies, surprise, 85
chocolate cream cheesecake, 85–86
chocolate mint pudding, 86
chocolate pie, 100–101
chocolate puffs, 87
chocolate-wafer mousse, 10
cider, hot mulled, 64
clam chowder, 154
clam dip, 58

cocktails
Daiquiri, 65
dry martini, 67
Mai Tai, 66
Manhattan, 66
Old-fashioned, 67

coconut recipes
  banana-coconut cream pie, 80
  golden peach teasers, 99
  Hawaiian ambrosia, 6
  macaroons, 87–88
  no-bake orange balls, 97
  pineapple mousse, 102
  toasted-coconut pie, 88
coffee, iced Russian, 63
cole slaw, 144
confetti snowball freeze, 89
cookies
  chocolate puffs, 87
  fortune kisses, 92–93
  mincemeat squares, 96
  never-fail cut-out, 91
  no-bake orange balls, 97
  nut macaroon wafers, 96–97
  pecan puffs, 22
  surprise chocolate cookies, 85
corn
  cream of, 14
  in hurry-up spaghetti, 141
  in Mexican party casserole, 116
  with pattypan squash, 160
corned beef and cabbage, 107
Cornish game hens
  and mushrooms, 125
  and rice, 34–35
cottage cheese recipes
  baked noodles Romanoff, 139

cottage cheese recipes (*cont.*)
  cranberry gelatin mold, 144
  frozen peach salad, 150
  scrambled eggs, 112
cottage pudding, raspberry, 102–103
crab Louis salad, 152
crabmeat fluff, 130–131
cracked wheat, *see* mock wild rice
cranberry gelatin mold, 144
cranberry-mold salad, 34
cranberry-orange relish, 136
  in gelatin mold, 144
cranberry-raspberry mold, 145
cranberry sauce with baked bananas, 79–80
cream cheese recipes
  cheese ball, 56
  chocolate cream cheesecake, 85–86
  creamy clam dip, 58
  cucumber-cream cheese logs, 58–59
  lemon-cheese pie, 94
cream-of-corn soup, 4
cream-of-cucumber salad, 145–146
crème brulée, custard, 90
crème de menthe-chocolate dessert, 89–90
creole meat loaf, 126
cucumber-cabbage salad, 38
cucumber-cream cheese logs, 58–59

cucumber salads, molded
  cream-of-cucumber, 145–
    146
  green aspic, 149
cup cakes, ice-cream-cone,
  106
custard crème brulée, 90
cut-out cookies, 91

Daiquiri cocktail, 65
Danish peanut cakes, 100
desserts, 75–106
  applesauce quickie, 47
  caramel-nut ice cream balls,
    14
  cherry graham-cracker pud-
    ding, 18
  chocolate-wafer mousse, 10
  Hawaiian ambrosia, 6
  lemon-gelatin pound cake,
    36
  pear surprise, 32
  pecan puffs, 22
  raspberry mold, 40
  strawberry gelatin mold,
    152–153
  upside-down peach cobbler,
    27
    See also frozen desserts
dips
  creamy clam, 58
  guacamole, 24
  onion, 146
Dutch red-cabbage-and-apple
  casserole, 30–31

egg recipes, 109–112
  cheese casserole, 16–17
  eggs Benedict, 50–51
  molded egg salad, 146
  spaghetti Troyer, 142
  spinach soufflé, 160–161
eggplant, shoestring, 43
eggs, baked, 109–110
eggs, scrambled, with cottage
  cheese, 112
eggs Benedict, 50–51
eggs Florentine, 111
Elkorn kidney-bean salad, 147
escalloped cauliflower, 6
escalloped ham and potatoes,
  20–21

fish recipes
  golden fish fry almondine,
    38–39
  salmon fluff, 130–131
  salmon wiggle, 131
  tuna casserole, 119
    See also seafood recipes
fish sauce (mustard-ketchup),
  25
fortune kisses, 92–93
frankfurter recipes
  glorified frankfurters, 30
  good goop, 127
French dip rolls, 72–73
French-fried onions, 159
French onion soup, 155
frostings, 91–92
  chocolate mint, for cup
    cakes, 106

onion-bacon crunch bread or rolls, 71
onion puffs, 60–61
onion soup, French, 155
onions
  French-fried, 159
  peas and, in salmon wiggle, 131
  scalloped, with peanut topping, 35
  in spring vegetable medley, 161–162
open-faced sandwiches
  cheese dreams, 70
  minced-chicken almondine, 74
  onion puffs, 60–61
orange balls, no-bake, 97
orange blossom rolls, 72
orange-cranberry relish, 136
  in cranberry gelatin mold, 144
orange crème, 98
oyster stew, 155

parfaits, 98–99
party recipes
  fortune kisses, 91–92
  guacamole dip, 24
  Hawaiian ambrosia, 6
  ice-cream-cone cup cakes, 106
  Mexican party casserole, 116

party recipes (cont.)
  minced-chicken sandwiches almondine, 74
  potato croquettes, 39
  salade niçoise, 12
  teriyaki strips, 55
pasta, see macaroni; noodles; spaghetti
pastry
  chocolate-chip, 84
  never-fail cut-out cookies, 91
  no-roll, 100–101
    See also graham-cracker recipes
pattypan squash filled with Mexicorn, 160
pea soup, split, 156
peach recipes
  frozen peach salad, 150
  golden peach teasers, 99
  ice cream parfait, 98–99
  pie, 100–101
  turnovers, 77–78
  upside-down cobbler, 27
peanut cakes, 100
peanuts with scalloped onions, 35
pear surprise, 31
peas
  with artichoke bottoms, 158
  and pearl onions in salmon wiggle, 131
  in vegetable medley, 162–163
pecan puffs, 22

pecans, recipes using
    cheese ball, 56
    fortune kisses, 92–93
peppers, green
    in barbecued shish kabobs,
        42
    in chicken almond, 122–123
    red-and-green-pepper salad,
        151
    with spaghetti, 142
Persian delight confection, 44
pie shell (no roll), 100–101
pies
    banana-coconut cream, 80
    deep-dish shrimp, 118
    fresh-strawberry, 103
    jiffy Boston cream, 81–82
    lemon-cheese, 94
    lemon-honey filling, 95
    pumpkin parfait, 101
    toasted-coconut, 88
        See also tarts; turn-
            overs
pilaff, 42–43
pineapple
    cole slaw with, 144
    in Hawaiian meatballs, 60
    juice in mulled cider, 63–
        64
    mousse, 102
    nibblers, 50
pizzas, tiny, 61
popovers, 26
pork
    chops with butter beans,
        114

pork (*cont.*)
    spareribs, 133
    steaks, breaded, 128
pot roast, 129–130
potato croquettes, 39
potato fans, oven-browned, 13
potato pancakes, 51
potato salad, hot German, 31
potato-sausage casserole, 115
potatoes
    and ham, escalloped, 20
    mashed, leftover, *see* mashed
        potatoes
    in New England clam chow-
        der, 154
    sweet-potato balls, 161
    sweet-potato fluff, 5–6
pound cake, lemon-gelatin, 36
puddings
    apple snow, 77
    cherry graham-cracker, 18
    chocolate mint, 86
    cottage, warm raspberry,
        102–103
    ready-to-eat, recipes using,
        81–82, 83–84, 85–86, 94–
        95, 100–101, 105
pumpkin desserts
    parfait pie, 101
    pie, 100–101
    turnovers, 77–78

raspberries
    with angel food cake, 76
    in parfait, 98–99